Birds of Zion National Park and Vicinity

Birds

of Zion National Park and Vicinity

Roland H. Wauer

Illustrated by
Mimi Hoppe Wolf

Foreword by
William H. Behle

Utah State University Press
Logan, Utah
1997

An earlier version of this book, co-authored by Roland H. Wauer and Dennis L. Carter, was published in 1965 by Zion Natural History Association. The author and publisher of this completely revised edition gratefully acknowledge Zion Natural History Association for permission to reproduce text and illustrations from that earlier edition.

Cover painting of a Canyon Wren and other cover illustrations by Mimi Hoppe Wolf

Typography by WolfPack
Cover design by Michelle Sellers

Printed in Canada

Wauer, Roland H.
    Birds of Zion National Park and vicinity / Roland H. Wauer ; illustrated by Mimi Wolf.
    p.   cm.
    Includes index.
    ISBN 0-87421-219-7
    1. Birds—Utah—Zion National Park. I. Title.
QL684.U8W3 1997
598.2972'48—dc20   96-35707
                                          CIP

TO JEROME GIFFORD

*for his many years of bird study
in Zion National Park and vicinity,
his desire for the truth, and for
providing a wonderful example to
the people of southwestern Utah*

Contents

Illustrations

Zion National Park

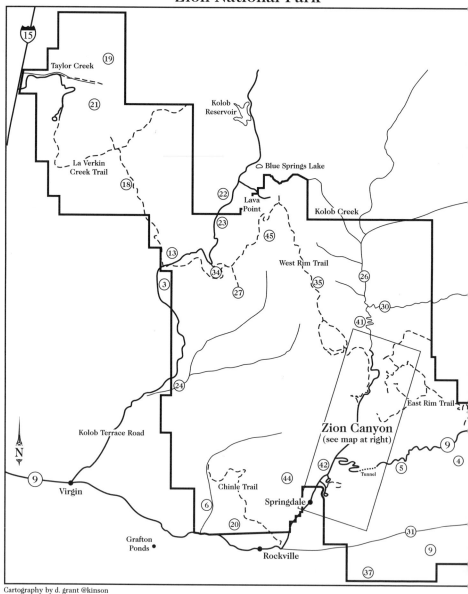

Cartography by d. grant @kinson

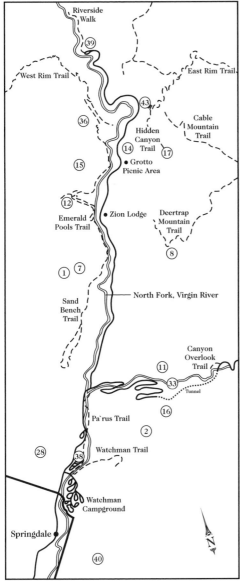

Riverside Walk

West Rim Trail

East Rim Trail

Cable Mountain Trail

Hidden Canyon Trail

Grotto Picnic Area

Emerald Pools Trail

Zion Lodge

Deertrap Mountain Trail

Sand Bench Trail

North Fork, Virgin River

Canyon Overlook Trail

Pa`rus Trail

Tunnel

Watchman Trail

Watchman Campground

Springdale

N

Cartography by d. grant @kinson

1	Birch Creek
2	Bridge Mountain
3	Cave Valley
4	Checkerboard Mesa
5	Clear Creek
6	Coalpits Wash
7	Court of the Patriarchs
8	Deertrap Mountain
9	Dennett Canyon
10	East Entrance
11	East Temple
12	Emerald Pools
13	Firepit Knoll
14	Great Whicte Throne
15	Heaps' Canyon
16	Hepworth Wash
17	Hidden Canyon
18	Hop Valley
19	Horse Ranch Mountain
20	Huber Wash
21	Kolob Canyons
22	Lamoreaux Ranch
23	Little Creek Valley
24	North Creek
25	North Fork Road
26	North Fork, Virgin River
27	Northgate Peaks
28	Oak Creek Canyon
29	Observation Piont
30	Orderville Canyon
31	Parunuweap Canyon
32	Pa`rus Trail
33	Pine Creek
34	Pine Valley
35	Potato Hollow
36	Refrigerator Canyon
37	Shunes Creek
38	South Campground
39	Temple of Sinawava
40	The Watchman
41	Virgin River Narrows
42	Visitor Center
43	Weeping Rock
44	West Temple
45	Wildcat Canyon

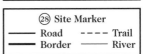

(28) Site Marker

——— Road   - - - - Trail
——— Border   ——— River

Foreword

WILLIAM H. BEHLE

I am very pleased to write the foreword to Ro Wauer's *Birds of Zion National Park and Vicinity*. This book will be valuable to professional ornithologists, those trying to document and obtain an understanding of Utah birdlife, as well as everyday birders who watch birds simply for the enjoyment.

This book is long overdue! *Birds of Zion National Park and Vicinity* is actually a revision of a book by the same title—by Roland H. Wauer and Dennis L. Carter—that was published by the Zion Natural History Association in 1965. That book has been out of print for more than a dozen years, and there has been nothing available to fill the vacuum since. But now Ro has completely rewritten the text after an extensive study of hundreds of bird sighting reports from 1964 through 1995. This new book includes 287 bird species, 54 more than the earlier work. This increase of almost 20% readily illustrates the value of Ro's new book.

I also am extremely pleased that Ro has dedicated this book to Jerome Gifford of Springdale, Utah. Jerome passed away in 1988 before he completed his own manuscript on the birds of the Zion Park area. He was a tireless birder, with true love for the park and its birdlife. Ro has very successfully incorporated all of Jerome's outstanding records into this new book.

There is no one more appropriate than Ro Wauer to write this book. Over the years he has written numerous books and articles about birds and nature in general. His *Field Guide to Birds of the Big*

Bend (Texas) is considered a classic birding field guide; he has recently completed four volumes on birding in all the national parks in the United States and Canada; and his *Naturalist's Mexico* and *Birder's Guide to the West Indies* are award-winners as well.

I first encountered Ro Wauer during the mid-1960s when he worked at Zion National Park as Assistant Chief Naturalist. He and Dennis Carter discovered birds in southwestern Utah that few ornithologists knew were there. In a sense, they made us aware of the ornithological importance of the southwestern corner of our state. From 1963 to mid-1966, Ro banded almost 6,000 individual birds of 102 species. He documented hundreds of migrants, many of which were new for the state, utilizing the Virgin River Valley. And finds like nesting Common Black-Hawks, Brown-crested Flycatchers, Summer Tanagers, and Rufous-crowned Sparrows helped us better understand Utah's avian diversity and fascinating biogeography.

Then, in late 1966, he moved on to an even better birding area: the Big Bend National Park in Texas, where, as Chief Park Naturalist for six years, he continued his study of birds. From there he moved to the position of Southwest Region Chief Scientist for six years, before accepting the position of Chief of Natural Resource Management in Washington, D.C.

After retiring from the National Park Service in 1989, Ro moved back to Texas where he has continued his study of birds and established a new career as a nature writer. *Birds of Zion National Park and Vicinity* is but one of nine books he has completed since.

I heartily recommend Ro's new book on Zion birds. Filled with wonderful, new information, it illustrates the author's love of nature, bird life, and Zion National Park, one of America's most remarkable natural wonders.

Introduction

Nothing can exceed the wonderous beauty of Little Zion Valley, which separates the two temples and their respective groups of towers. . . . In its proportions it is about equal to Yosemite, but in the nobility and beauty of the sculptures there is no comparison. No wonder the fierce Mormon zealot, who named it, was reminded of the Great Zion, on which his fervid thoughts were bent—'of houses not built with hands, eternal in the heavens.

—CLARENCE DUTTON, 1872

Zion National Park is geographically located in the southwestern corner of the greater Colorado Plateau, which extends north and east through Utah to central Colorado. More specifically, Zion's abundant canyons cut into the Kolob Terrace of the Markagunt Plateau, which is on the southwestern terrace of the Colorado Plateau.

Zion's highlands, which rise above the arid lowlands like "islands in the sky," are mantled with a green forest of pines and firs. Below the high towers and mesas are hundreds of canyons that extend into the warm deserts to the southwest. The grandest of these canyons is Zion Canyon, which appears to have its feet in the lowlands and its head in the sky. There is a 5,100-foot difference in elevation between the desert communities in the park's southwestern corner and the northern highlands.

Zion Canyon and the many other canyons offer a twisting maze of diversity, where cool, protected niches of highland vegetation often lie below arid slopes dominated by desert plants. Scattered throughout are extensive, colorful sandstone areas that are relatively bare of vegetation. These are interlaced by numerous streams and highland valleys that possess thick riparian woodlands, dense thickets of oaks, or forest communities of pine, fir, and aspen.

This varied environment has, so far, produced a total of 287 bird species; 35 of those have not yet been fully verified (by a specimen or reported by five or more individuals or parties) and are included in a list of hypothetical species. Of the 252 fully accepted species, 133 (53%) are known to nest; 36 species (14%) are permanent residents; and 97 (38%) have been found only in summer. Seventy-nine (31% of 252) of the 133 nesting species are neotropical migrants, which are birds that winter south of the U.S.–Mexico Border— sometimes as far south as Central or South America—and nest north of the border. A total of 142 species (56%) are migrants, passing through the Zion Park area in spring and/or fall; 38 of those have been recorded as "migrant only." Thirty-one of the 142 migrants have been recorded only in spring, while three species have been found only in the fall, which is good evidence of the influence of the Virgin River Valley as a northbound migration route. In addition, 138 (55%) species are present during the winter months; only seven of those have been recorded in the Zion Park area solely in winter.

Ornithological Park History

The first significant published record of bird study in Zion was Clifford C. Presnall's checklist in 1935, "The Birds of Zion National Park" in the *Proceedings of the Utah Academy of Sciences, Arts, and Letters*. Presnall utilized field notes of many early Zion Park naturalists— including Vasco M. Tanner, Angus M. Woodbury, Gordon Y. Croft, and Stephen D. Durrant—and examined bird specimens from several institutions in preparing a list of 140 species. The next important study of Zion birds was Russell K. Grater's *The Birds of Zion, Bryce, and Cedar Breaks, Utah*, published in 1947. Grater discussed only the common birds (98 species) but listed an additional 67 birds, totaling 165 species.

Increased interest in birds during the late 1950s and early 1960s by Dennis L. Carter, Richard C. Russell, Roland H. Wauer, and several others, added to the park's avian information base. A 1965 book, *Birds of Zion National Park and Vicinity*, by Wauer and Carter, included a total of 233 species.

Since 1965, several individuals have provided additional bird records, increasing the park's database and expanding the species list even further. The most productive individual during this period was Jerome Gifford, to whom I have dedicated this book. Jerome maintained almost daily records on birds found throughout the Zion Park area, especially in the lower canyons. He also undertook a series of breeding bird censuses at varied locations, from Coalpits Wash to Lava Point, and several of these sites also were censused in winter. Finally, he prepared an annotated list of all the known species (Gifford 1987); that manuscript was never completed due to his untimely death in 1988.

My involvement with this book was largely due to the initial suggestion and encouragement of Vic Vieira, Zion Park's Chief of Resource Management and Research. But once I agreed to undertake the task, principal support was provided by Natural Resource Specialist Sheri Fedorchak.

During my visit to Zion National Park in September and October 1995, when I was gathering information for this book (actually a rewrite of the 1965 book), I was permitted to examine Jerome's notes and manuscript. And Jewel Gifford, Jerome's sister, graciously allowed me to utilize his material with no restrictions.

This new book, therefore, is largely the result of Jerome's love for birds and his significant efforts to document their presence and status. It is designed to help the reader find the various birds during each season of the year. It is not, however, designed to aid in bird identification; there are numerous excellent field guides already available. Using one of the field guides, along with this book, it is possible to find and identify as many as 50 to 60 bird species in a single day.

Acknowledgments

Several individuals at Zion National Park provided considerable support and encouragement for this project. I am grateful to them all. Sheri Fedorchak was extremely helpful; she continuously went out of her way to assist with area logistics, obtaining all available records, coordinating the park's review of my manuscript, and doing a number of other chores that arose. Several other park employees provided additional assistance in one way or another: Frank Cope, Steve Holder, Eddie Lopez, and Vic Vieira helped with logistical support; Dan Cohan, Brent Hetzler, Mary Hunnicutt, Carolyn Sandlin, Darla Sidles, and David Sinton helped gather reference materials; and Denny Davies, Sheri Fedorchak, Mary Hunnicutt, Shane Pruett, and Debbie Wong reviewed the final manuscript.

I also thank Steven Hedges, birder and biologist living in Cedar City, Utah, and Clayton M. White, professor of zoology at Brigham Young University, for their very thorough reviews of my manuscript, which resulted in numerous worthwhile suggestions, and Steven Hedges for responding to various queries and requests.

Jewel Gifford of Springdale also allowed me to examine and utilize her brother's extensive database (see introduction for more). I am most grateful to her.

There also is a long list of individuals who, over the years, have provided the park with one to numerous bird sighting reports (National Park Service [NPS] files, Zion National Park). The book would not have been possible without their contributions. These birders include Del Armstrong, Glen Arnold, Louise Arnold, Scott Ashman, Hugh and Marsha Bain, Lynn Ballard, Paul Bauer, Jurt Baumgarten, Lewis Beatty, Cindy Beaudett, Jill Blumenthal, Katie Bode, Lars Boll, Robert Bond, Rick Boretti, Terry Boykie, Josh Brack, Andrea Brand, Marc Breuninger, Mike Britten, Mark Bromley, Phil Brouse, M. Callister, E. H. Cantrell, Jr., Dennis Carter, Greer Chesher, Robert Clark, Allegra Collister, Frank Cope, Andrew Core, Fern and J. L. Crawford, Glenn and Meridy Cross, Brenda Cunningham, Denny and Gail Davies, Jack Davis, Jerry Davis, Nancy and Robert Dean, Christine and Jon Dick, Dale Dockstader, Peter Dring, John Egbert, Janet Ellis, Austin Excell, David Excell, Louise Excell, Kris Fair, Don and Carole Falvey, Rich and Sheri Fedorchak, Cathy and Clifford Felix, Richard Fesler, Joel Fishbein, William Fisher, Leah and Richard Foerster, Nancy Fonicello, James Fraley, Myrna Fraley, R. Fridell, Alice Galleys, Heather Gates, Ward Gibson, Dane Gifford, F. D. Gifford, Jerome Gifford, Jewel Gifford, Lance Gifford, Raymond Gifford, Jennifer Gillette, Tom Gillette, Roy Given, Gordon Gover, Kate Grandison, Earl and Margaret Grant, Henry Grantham, Russell Grater, Patsy Graves, Jeff Gubler, Valeria Haan, Dan Habig, Allan Hagood, Joseph A. Hall, Wayne Hamilton, Clyde and Lois Harden, Jan Hart, Erik Haskell, Jim Haycock, Frank Hays, Larry Hays, Michael Hays, Steve Hedges, J. Hertman, Brent Hetzler, Kathy Heyder, M. Hilkey, Ned Hill, Robert Hudson, Mary Hunnicutt, Catherine Inman, Victor Jackson, Carl Jepson, Ray Johnson, Pearl Justet, Jeff Kamps, Ivan Kassovic, Allan R. Keith, Ken Kertell, Steve King, Hugh Kingery, Rene Lauback, Jeanne LeBer, V. E. Lemert, Leon Lewis, W. S. Long, Frank Loskot, Vincent Lu, Rudy Lueck, Barbara Lund, Dan Lundeen, Tasha MacIlreen, Dr. and Mrs. Otto Mackerson, Melanie Madsen, Jim Maender, Nelson Maloney, Tim Manns, David Matt, Catherine Matthews, C. McCollum, ? McDowell, Ladessa Miller, David and Margaret Mindell, Debbie Monago, Bruce Moorhead, Don Morris, Clyde Morrison, Jonathan Moser, Vince Mowbray, J. R. Murphy, Guy Musser, Raymond Mustoe, Laird Naylor, Jon Nelson, M. Nelson, Riley Nelson, David Ng, Scott Nichols, Samantha Niergarth, Frank Oberhansley, R. J. O'Brien, Sheldon Olson, Vickie Parkinson, Cathy Pasterezyk, Judy Perkins, Joyce and Seth Phalen, Rupert Pilkington, Clifford Presnall, Shane

Pruett, Kurt Ranslem, Bob Rhodes, Robert Rucker, Dick Russell, Terry Sadler, V. Scheidt, Liesl Schindler, Harry Schneider, S. Schneider, Peter Scott, Alan Seagert, Don and Martha Shearer, Keith Sherman, Melissa Siders, Darla Sidles, M. M. Simmons, David Sinton, C. R. Skelton, Denver and Myrtle Smith, Ray Smith, Matt Snyder, Phillip Sollins, Ella and Richard Sorensen, Dorothy Sousa, Monica Speidel, Janice and Scott Staats, Neal Stephens, Ellen Strauss, Richard A. Stuart, Priscilla and Steve Summers, Harvey and Karen Swainse, Vasco Tanner, Jim and Shirley Thielen, Tim Tibbetts, Clarence Todd, Kirk Topham, Charles Torrance, Gene Trapp, James Tucker, Robert Tweit, Betty and Frank Urban, James Van Sickel, Judy Vavra, John Voyles, Al Walent, Kevin Wallace, Merrill Webb, Jack and Phyliss Wilburn, David Willey, Ray Williams, Victor Willis, F. Winch, Doyle Winder, Lois Winter, Robert Wood, Angus Woodbury, R. Woodward, Eunice Yager, Andy Young, and Mark Zolink.

In addition, Dr. William H. Behle, professor emeritus at the University of Utah and the state's most highly regarded ornithologist, kindly agreed to prepare the foreword to this book. Dr. Behle has had a long-term interest in the birds of Zion National Park and vicinity, and his support for this book, as well as the earlier one that I wrote with my friend and colleague Dennis Carter, is much appreciated.

The Canyon Wren painting on the cover and all the pen-and-ink sketches were done by Mimi Wolf. Her 35 illustrations greatly enhance this book, and I am most grateful to her for her extraordinary talent and cooperative spirit.

Also, I am grateful to Howard Rollin for the four full-page paintings of Zion Park's principal bird communities. These illustrations were done for the earlier edition of the book that appeared in 1965. Howard has since passed away. I am pleased to use them once again.

Finally, I want to thank my wife, Betty: she not only provided considerable support for undertaking this project, she also accompanied me on my park visit, serving as traveling companion, chief cook, and bottle-washer.

Plant and Animal Communities

Zion National Park and vicinity contain a wide variety of plant and animal communities, representing three rather distinct regions of the West and Southwest: the Colorado Plateau to the east, the Great Basin to the west of the Kolob Canyons, and the Mojave Desert to the southwest. Botanist Kimball Harper, in a 1988 vegetation study of the Zion Park area, identified 10 rather distinct vegetation types based on dominant plant species. The 10 types include blackbrush, sagebrush, pinyon-juniper, mountain brush, rock crevice plants, ponderosa pine, mixed conifer, riparian, hanging gardens, and introduced species assemblages on heavily disturbed former fields.

I have further simplified Harper's 10 vegetative categories to six rather distinct communities that best relate to the park's avian distribution. These six communities—Desert, Riparian Woodland, Pinyon-Juniper Woodland, High Country, High Cliffs, and Water Areas—are described below.

The Desert

Although the word *desert* means many things to many people, it refers here to the arid lowlands that lie below the pinyon-juniper woodlands, generally below 4,500 feet elevation, and mostly in the southwestern corner of the park. However, extended fingers of desert vegetation may reach far into the lower canyons on south-facing

1

slopes and on even higher flats with sandy, dry soils that experience extended periods of sunlight. The extensive desert communities in the lowlands generally are characterized by treeless washes and slopes.

Typical desert plants include the sand sagebrush, honey mesquite, creosote bush, saltbush, and blackbrush. The best examples of this community occur in Coalpits and Huber Washes, Parunuweap Canyon, Shunes Creek, and on the open flats in lower Zion Canyon.

The heaviest bird concentration in the desert occurs during the spring months, especially during migration. Breeding bird populations, although rather sparse, can be highly vocal and active during late March, April, and early May. Desert birds move to higher elevations or are usually silent after nesting, but the area once again is popular during the winter months. Typical breeding birds of the desert include the Gambel's Quail, Greater Roadrunner, Costa's Hummingbird, Say's Phoebe, Rock Wren, Black-throated Sparrow, and House Finch.

The Riparian Woodland

This is the lush woodland that occurs along the rivers and streams in the lower canyons and side-canyons of the park. It is characterized by broadleaf trees—such as cottonwood, boxelder, and ash—various orchard trees, and a ground cover of silty soils and debris from the flooding watercourses. Most of Zion Canyon, including the Watchman and South Campgrounds and the vicinity of the Zion Lodge and Grotto Picnic Area, are dominated by this community.

The Virgin River streamsides, like the surrounding desert, extend far to the southwest of the park, and many birds utilize this environment as a convenient pathway during their spring and (to a much lesser degree) fall migration.

Throughout most of the year, the riparian woodland is Zion's most popular bird community. Typical breeding birds include the Great Horned Owl, Black-chinned Hummingbird, Hairy Woodpecker, Black-capped Chickadee, American Robin, Warbling Vireo, Black-headed Grosbeak, and Bullock's Oriole.

The Pinyon-Juniper Woodland

Above the desert and below the rim of the high mesas exists a community of short evergreens, oaks, and open sage flats; the abundant pinyon-juniper woodlands are sometimes called "pygmy forest," due to their short stature. Juniper is most common in the lower reaches of the woodland, pinyon pine dominates at higher elevations, and stands of Gambel's oak occur in protected canyons and along the upper edges of the woodland. Interspersed among the trees are small-to-large tracts of big sagebrush. Other common plants of this woodland include mountain mahogany, cliffrose, serviceberry, and scrub oak. The pinyon-juniper woodland is the most extensive community within the Zion National Park area.

Examples of pinyon-juniper woodland occur below the cliffs of Navajo Sandstone in Zion Canyon and on the warmer slopes in the mid-elevation canyons and valleys. During the spring and summer months, this community is an important nesting area for birds; it is only moderately important in winter. Typical breeding birds include the Broad-tailed Hummingbird, Ash-throated Flycatcher, Western Scrub-Jay, Plain Titmouse, Bushtit, Blue-gray Gnatcatcher, Gray Vireo, and Black-throated Gray Warbler.

The High Country

All of the land above the pinyon-juniper woodland may be regarded as high country. This includes the "sky islands," the forested areas atop the high towers, as well as the more extensive areas in mid-elevation valleys and on the higher terraces and mesas of the plateau. Each offers a slight variation in its vegetation. Ponderosa pine dominates the warmer parts of the high country, and big sagebrush flats persist throughout. Aspen, white fir, and Douglas fir occur in the cooler canyons and niches and on the higher terraces. Dense forests of pine, fir, and aspen occur wherever there is the right combination of terrain, soil, cool temperatures, and moisture, such as in Potato Hollow.

Zion's high country can best be reached from the North Fork Road and from the Kolob Terrace (Kolob Reservoir) Road; the East and West Rim Trails offer hiking access to the higher terraces from

Zion Canyon. This highland environment supports a large bird population during the summer and fall months but a very sparse one in winter. Representative breeding birds include the Steller's Jay, Mountain Chickadee, White-breasted and Pygmy Nuthatches, and Grace's Warbler.

The High Cliffs

Few communities are as impressive as the abundant high cliffs of Zion National Park. These largely bare sandstone areas, which literally dominate the park's natural scene, support several bird species that are either numerous or a dominating member of the area. Typical breeding species include the Red-tailed Hawk, Golden Eagle, American Kestrel, Peregrine Falcon, White-throated Swift, Violet-green and Cliff Swallows, Common Raven, and Rock and Canyon Wrens.

The Water Areas

Water areas in Zion National Park and vicinity are limited in number and size. Although seeps and springs occur throughout, they are relatively scarce. In the lowlands, the Virgin River is a dominant feature, and the river, side-streams, springs, and seeps are relatively significant to the park's bird ecology, despite the fact that they cover a very small portion of the entire area. The small ponds that occur in Springdale, Rockville, Grafton, on North Creek, and in Shunes Creek have produced numerous bird sightings of note.

Although very few birds nest in the water areas, the vicinity of the ponds is a good place to find birds, especially in spring and fall. Typical migrants that may be found at these lowland water areas include the Great Blue Heron, American Avocet, Spotted Sandpiper, Common Snipe, and several kinds of ducks. The Green-winged Teal, Mallard, Northern Pintail, and Belted Kingfisher can be expected in winter. Breeding birds known to utilize this habitat in the lowlands include the Mallard, Killdeer, Spotted Sandpiper, Virginia Rail, Belted Kingfisher, and Common Yellowthroat.

Important water areas in the highlands are the Kolob Reservoir, Blue Springs Lake, and a series of small ponds below the reservoir. These wetlands are most productive in summer and during migration, but freezing occurs in winter. Typical breeding birds of the high-country lakes and ponds include the Green-winged and Cinnamon Teal, Mallard, Killdeer, and Spotted Sandpiper.

Bird Finding

Birds are mobile creatures that move from place to place to find essential food, water, and shelter. Although migrants are most mobile, often appearing in out-of-ordinary places, the breeding birds generally are limited to particular habitats. There they defend their territories, court their mates, nest, and raise their young. While nesting, they rarely occur elsewhere. Therefore, to find a bird of your choice it is important to understand what habitat is preferred. Water birds, migrants or not, usually frequent water areas, while most songbirds prefer terrestrial habitats; and each selects preferred sites. One should not expect to find a Greater Roadrunner in the dense pine-fir forests or a Red Crossbill in the desert. You should not look for a Mallard or teal among the rock-strewn slopes of Coalpits Wash or a Gambel's Quail at Potato Hollow. A few species, however, such as the Turkey Vulture and Mourning Dove, seem to utilize a wide range of habitats from the desert lowlands to the highlands.

The Migration

The first sign of the spring migration at Zion National Park may be detected by the departure of some of the birds that have been wintering in the lower canyons. Most noticeable is the decline in Dark-eyed Juncos; they begin to move up the canyons and into the higher valleys as early as mid-February. A sudden snowstorm may force them back to warmer locations, and some years a "tidal" effect of birds moving back and forth with each cold front can be detected.

The filtering of birds through the canyons and lower valleys is hardly noticeable at first, but by mid-March it is very evident that the bird population is again on the upswing. Warm and sunny days are filled with birdsongs, and swallows and swifts hunt insects along the canyons and washes. By the time the first vireo song is heard on an April morning, the northbound migration is well underway. The actual movement of individual birds through the Zion Park area is not easy to detect. The continuous flow can be detected very well at a feeding station or as a result of banding, but the best evidence of migration can be realized if there is a severe storm in the high country. Such a sudden change in temperature and visibility may send literally thousands of migrating birds into the lower canyons to seek refuge and enough food to keep their bodies warm and alive. At times like these, the desert areas and open flats in the protected canyons swarm with birds. As many as 50 to 60 bird species may be found then, including many species that rarely visit the lowlands.

A good example of such a storm is one that occurred in early May 1964. Snow fell through the night and by morning the ground was white; food for birds was drastically reduced. Dozens of dead birds were found throughout the canyons, but thousands survived by finding warmer temperatures and available food at lower elevations. The most common survivors were Mountain Bluebirds, American Robins, various warblers, Green-tailed Towhees, Dark-eyed (Gray-headed) Juncos, and Pine Siskins. Surprisingly, three Flammulated Owls were found at the visitor center and nearby that day and the next. They were banded and released. The sudden appearance of this highland nester in the lowlands makes one wonder how many more of these normally rare owls found shelter among the canyons of Zion during that particular storm.

Similar periods of inclement weather may occur several times each spring and occasionally in the fall. This influx of birds into the lowlands is also noticeable during the winter to a lesser extent. Juncos and White-crowned Sparrows, which begin to move up the slopes with a few days of warm weather, will return to their regular wintering grounds immediately if a sudden cold front reaches the area. As spring progresses, this altitudinal movement becomes more pronounced until the winter birds finally disappear altogether. Bird finding during the spring, fall, and winter months is usually best on days of inclement weather and shortly thereafter. The last spring migrant to arrive on its nesting grounds is the Western Wood-Pewee. Then, its songs seem to fill the canyons and valleys from the riparian woodland to the high country. By late May, almost all of the northbound movement has ceased, but it is only a few short weeks before the southward trend begins. Such early southbound migrants as the Rufous Hummingbird can be expected in the highlands by late June or early July.

It also is the time of year that post-nesting birds begin their autumnal wanderings that may take them far from their breeding grounds and, sometimes, far from their preferred habitats. A few of the wanderers and fall transients that may appear in Zion Park and vicinity include the Northern Harrier, Lesser Nighthawk, Lewis' Woodpecker, Pinyon Jay, Clark's Nutcracker, Northern Mockingbird, Sage Thrasher, American Pipit, and Sage Sparrow.

The southward migration is well underway by mid-September and continues until the first snowfall in the high country. During fall months with mild temperatures and light precipitation, there is little evidence of the southward movement in the lowlands. However, a storm is likely to bring the feathered evidence of migration into the lowlands. And a visit to the highlands in October will make one well aware of the extent of the fall migration.

The annual spring and fall movements of birds—between their wintering and breeding grounds—are some of the most exciting periods of the year. Neotropical migrants, such as the vireos and warblers, return to their North American nesting sites from as far away as Mexico and Central America. Other species, such as the juncos and some sparrows, may move only from the desert lowlands onto the forested highlands. Whereas birds that nest in the desert habitat may return as early as February, high country nesters may not arrive until May or June.

Birds generally follow set patterns of movement during their annual treks. The neotropical migrants often utilize major flyways that extend north and south across North America. Although Zion National Park is not located on a major flyway, secondary flyways extend along both edges of the Markagunt Plateau. The extended north/south depression west of the plateau, between Cedar City and St. George and southward, is recognized as a relatively important migration route, especially for southbound migrants. The Sevier River drainage, to the east of the park, and the lower Virgin River and Parunuweap Canyon drainages, within the southwestern corner of the park, are less important. Overall, however, the Virgin River pathway is a strong influence on northbound migrants.

The Spring Months

More birds may be found in Zion National Park and vicinity in the late spring and early summer than at any other time of the year. This is when the high country nesters arrive on their breeding grounds and the lowland birds are well along in their nesting cycle. Spring also is one of the best times of the year to visit Zion National Park; the broadleaf trees in the lowlands are in full foliage, and the flowers are at their blooming peak.

A walk into the DESERT area may result in the realization that this low, arid environment is actually full of life. Springtime in the desert can be very exciting. Coalpits Wash is at its peak in May. Most evident are the House Finches that nest on the cholla cacti and saltbushes. Their songs echo from each high point where they sit and watch for an intruder to their territory.

The Gambel's Quail raises broods along the lower part of the wash, and an occasional Greater Roadrunner may be seen carrying home a lizard or snake to a waiting family. The whistling hiss of a diving Costa's Hummingbird male, loudest at the bottom of its dive, can be expected as well. The plaintive call of the Say's Phoebe cannot be mistaken. The rocky ledges along the mouth of Coalpits Wash offer choice nesting sites for this flycatcher, which seems to have no territorial disputes with Northern Rough-winged Swallows that utilize similar nesting localities throughout the desert portion of the park.

In addition, you cannot walk far along Coalpits Wash in spring without hearing the single-pitched trill of the Rock Wren. Its loud song echoes along the wash and blends nicely with the sweet songs of Black-throated Sparrows. The blackbrush and saltbushes offer good nesting sites for this attractive little sparrow. The RIPARIAN WOODLAND is, literally, alive with birds during the spring months. An early morning walk through the campgrounds and almost anywhere in Zion Canyon will convince anyone that this habitat is an important one for nesting birds. One of the park's most productive routes—the Pa'rus Trail—is found between the Watchman Campground and Zion Canyon Junction. This trail runs along the riparian corridor, crosses the river several times, and parallels the large grassy flat between the river and Bridge Mountain.

The air above the treetops is often filled with fast-flying Violet-green Swallows and White-throated Swifts. The swallows nest at all elevations in the park, while the black-and-white swifts nest in crevices on the cliffs throughout the canyons of Zion; both hunt insects along the waterways. Other insect-eating birds may be seen as they dash out from the treetops in pursuit of a tasty tidbit. Watch for Western Kingbirds in the lower parts of the area and Cordilleran Flycatchers in the cooler side-canyons.

You cannot walk far along the canyon trails without hearing the insistent calls of Western Wood-Pewees and the whistle-songs of Solitary and Warbling Vireos. Both vireos nest among the foliage of the cottonwoods and other broadleaf trees throughout the canyon and into the higher valleys. Here, too, may be found the Black-chinned Hummingbird, Bushtit, Black-headed Grosbeak, Bullock's Oriole, and Lesser Goldfinch. The Black-headed Grosbeak is one of Zion's most common spring and summer residents; you are likely to find it at the campgrounds, the Zion Lodge, and the Temple of Sinawava.

The many shrubs and small trees along the streams provide nesting sites for the Yellow Warbler, Lazuli Bunting, and Song Sparrow, and the Yellow-breasted Chat and Blue Grosbeak occur at localized areas in the lower portions of the canyons.

Several of the riparian woodland breeding birds are cavity nesters that utilize cracks, loose bark, and holes in the trees. Most common are the Hairy Woodpecker, Northern (red-shafted) Flicker, and House Wren; below Springdale, the Lucy's Warbler can be added to this group of nesters.

The Brown-headed Cowbird also is a spring resident of the riparian woodland and often can be seen searching the vegetation for other birds' nests in which the female may lay her eggs. Foster parents, usually much smaller birds, will raise the huge babies—and these babies may completely dominate the nest and feeding.

Nesting activity in the PINYON-JUNIPER WOODLAND can be almost as great as that in the riparian woodland. Breeding birds are most obvious in May and June, and some of the best localities for bird finding in this habitat are along the Watchman Trail and the lower parts of the Kolob Terrace Road.

A walk up the Watchman Trail offers a good sampling of the birds that nest in this habitat. The lower portion of the trail contains rocky terrain and open ledges; juniper is dominant. You cannot walk far without hearing the beautiful descending and decelerating songs of Canyon Wrens. No other bird typifies Zion National Park so well as this little songster; it normally is abundant on the talus slopes in Zion Canyon and in rocky canyons throughout the park. You also may see Rock Wrens on the rock-strewn slopes and about the ledges. Also watch for Say's Phoebes and Ash-throated Flycatchers; these species nest on the rocky ledges.

During the evenings, listen for the plaintive calls of the Common Poorwill. This nightjar is most often seen along the roadways at night; its red eyes show up well in the headlights of vehicles. You will seldom find this nocturnal bird during the daylight, but occasionally it is disturbed on a brushy slope or open ledge where it may be nesting on the bare ground.

A sparse woodland begins a short distance up the slope, and a heavier woodland of pinyon pines exists along the upper half of the Watchman Trail. The Mourning Dove, Black-headed Grosbeak, and Spotted Towhee are common here during spring and summer and may be found along the entire length of the trail. The little Black-chinned Hummingbird constructs a thimble-sized nest on a twig or branch; and cavity-nesters utilizing this area include the Hairy Woodpecker, Northern (red-shafted) Flicker, Ash-throated Flycatcher, and Plain Titmouse.

One of the most numerous birds of the pinyon-juniper woodland is the Western Scrub-Jay. Its loud squawks can often be heard throughout the woodland. Listen, too, for the scolding calls of the Bewick's and House Wrens and the Blue-gray Gnatcatcher. All three species nest here and usually are heard before they are seen.

Less vociferous when nesting is the Bushtit that builds a long bas-ket-shaped nest among the tree foliage.

During May and early June, an intermingling of many birdsongs can be heard along the trail. With experience, one can pick out the songs of Gray, Solitary, and Warbling Vireos; Virginia's and Black-throated Gray Warblers; Black-headed Grosbeak; and Spotted Towhee. And, with a little patience and a sharp eye, these perky songbirds may also be seen.

The HIGH COUNTRY is still cold and wintry during the first of spring when nesting begins in the desert areas of the park. By late May, however, the high country nesters have arrived on their breed-ing grounds, and the forests of pine and fir echo with birdsong.

The ponderosa pine forest offers the birder a wide variety of bird species, and a spring day spent along the West Rim Trail or in the forest accessible by the North Fork Road or Kolob Terrace Road may result in the finding of 45 to 55 species of birds. Two in particular may be found here that are not found elsewhere in the park during the nesting season: Pygmy Nuthatch and Grace's Warbler. You sometimes must search the tall ponderosa pines for a view of either bird, although the calls of the Pygmy Nuthatch and the sweet songs of Grace's Warbler can be heard for a considerable distance.

The ponderosa pine forest community also contains cliffs and sagebrush flats. The cliffs are utilized as nesting sites by several large birds. Watch for the Turkey Vulture, Red-tailed Hawk, Golden Eagle, and Peregrine and Prairie Falcons. The lower sagebrush flats provide nesting sites for the Lark Sparrow, the higher sagebrush flats are utilized by Brewer's and Vesper Sparrows, and the brushy edges support nesting Green-tailed Towhees and Chipping Sparrows.

Potato Hollow, along the upper portion of the West Rim Trail, is a beautiful depression filled with ponderosa pine, aspen, white fir, and Douglas fir. A walk through this little valley in early June may result in the finding of most of the typical high country breeding birds. In the forest watch for Sharp-shinned and Cooper's Hawks; Band-tailed Pigeons; Broad-tailed Hummingbirds; Red-naped Sapsuckers; Hairy and Downy Woodpeckers; Northern (red-shafted) Flickers; Western Wood-Pewees; Violet-green Swallows; Steller's Jays; Black-capped and Mountain Chickadees; Red-breasted, White-breasted, and Pygmy Nuthatches; Ruby-crowned Kinglets; Western and Mountain

Pictorial Guide to Plant and Animal Communities

Great White Throne from Zion Canyon; photo by Roland H. Wauer

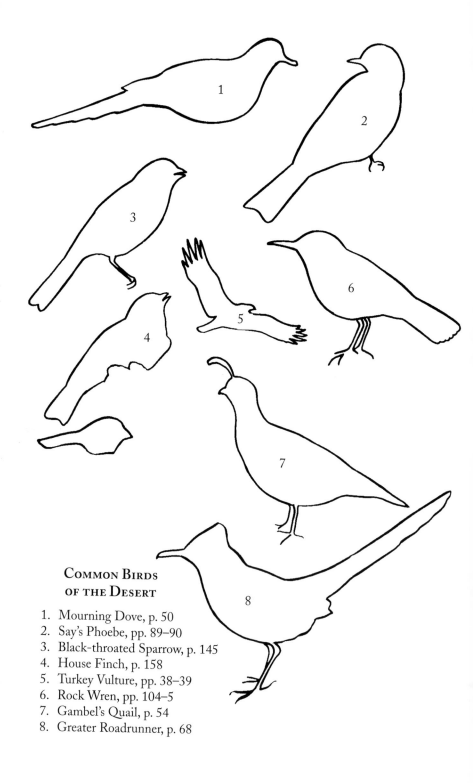

COMMON BIRDS
OF THE DESERT

The desert environment of Coalpits Wash, looking south toward the Virgin River floodplain; photo by Roland H. Wauer

Riparian woodland habitat along the Virgin River, from near the visitor center; photo by Roland H. Wauer

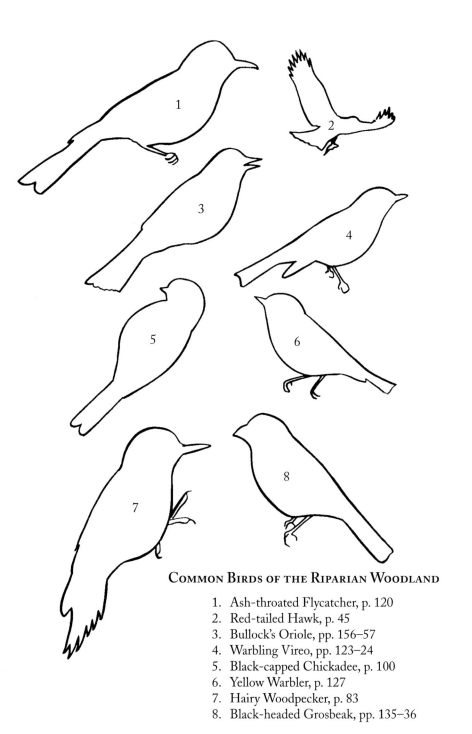

COMMON BIRDS OF THE RIPARIAN WOODLAND

1. Ash-throated Flycatcher, p. 120
2. Red-tailed Hawk, p. 45
3. Bullock's Oriole, pp. 156–57
4. Warbling Vireo, pp. 123–24
5. Black-capped Chickadee, p. 100
6. Yellow Warbler, p. 127
7. Hairy Woodpecker, p. 83
8. Black-headed Grosbeak, pp. 135–36

Massive cliffs of the Great West Canyon, from along the West Rim Trail; photo by Roland H. Wauer

Pinyon-juniper woodland from the Kolob Reservoir road; photo by Roland H. Wauer

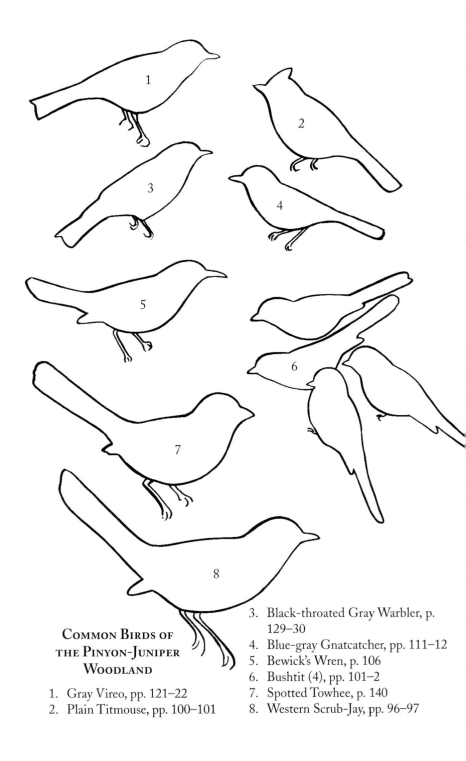

Common Birds of the Pinyon-Juniper Woodland

1. Gray Vireo, pp. 121–22
2. Plain Titmouse, pp. 100–101
3. Black-throated Gray Warbler, p. 129–30
4. Blue-gray Gnatcatcher, pp. 111–12
5. Bewick's Wren, p. 106
6. Bushtit (4), pp. 101–2
7. Spotted Towhee, p. 140
8. Western Scrub-Jay, pp. 96–97

Blue Springs Lake from along the Kolob Reservoir road; photo by Roland H. Wauer

Ponderosa pine woodland in the high country along the Kolob Reservoir road; photo by Roland H. Wauer

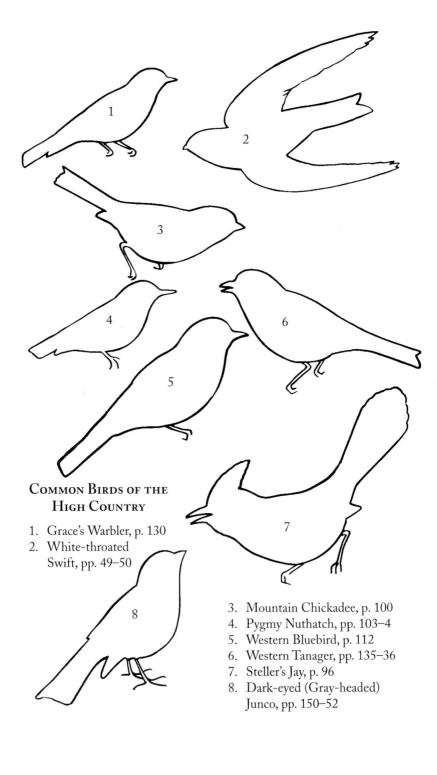

COMMON BIRDS OF THE HIGH COUNTRY

An October view southwest toward Zion Canyon from Lava Point; photo by Roland H. Wauer

Bluebirds; Townsend's Solitaires; Hermit Thrushes; American Robins; Solitary and Warbling Vireos; Orange-crowned, Virginia's, and Grace's Warblers; Western Tanager; Dark-eyed (Gray-headed) Juncos; Cassin's Finches; and Pine Siskins.

A seep exists at the edge of Potato Hollow but becomes dry by midsummer. The willows and other wetland plants provide nesting sites for Dusky Flycatchers; Orange-crowned, Yellow, and MacGillivray's Warblers; and Lincoln's Sparrows. The willow patches about the open meadows, such as those in the vicinity of Blue Springs Lake and Kolob Reservoir, offer nesting sites for Brewer's Blackbirds as well.

The WATER AREAS of Zion Park and vicinity are of minor importance as nesting sites. In Zion Canyon, all of the breeding birds that utilize this habitat may be found by visiting the Virgin River between Rockville and Springdale and walking the riverside trails near the Zion Lodge, Grotto Picnic Area, and above the Temple of Sinawava. Within the town of Springdale, as well as along North Creek, are ponds that contain a swamp-like environment. Spring nesters utilizing these areas include the Killdeer, Black Phoebe, Yellow Warbler, Common Yellowthroat, Red-winged Blackbird, and Song Sparrow. And a morning stroll on the Riverside Walk (above the Temple of Sinawava) and beyond is likely to produce the Spotted Sandpiper and American Dipper. As many as four to five Dipper nests may be discovered during a day's trip down the Virgin River Narrows.

In the high country, the ponds along Little and Kolob Creeks, Blue Springs Lake, and the Kolob Reservoir all offer available nesting sites for various birds, including Green-winged and Cinnamon Teal, Mallards, Killdeer, and Spotted Sandpipers.

The Summer Months

Summer is the time of year when human visitation to Zion National Park is highest, but it is not the best time of year for finding birds. Because of Zion's proximity to the southern deserts, summer daytime temperatures in the lowlands may be as high as 95 to 105 degrees Fahrenheit. On the other hand, temperatures on the Kolob Terrace are ideal during summer. Many of the lowland birds, therefore, move to more comfortable surroundings at higher elevations once their breeding cycle is complete. This post-nesting movement results in a major depopulation of birds in the lowlands and a defined increase in the highlands.

The DESERT environment retains only a trace of its springtime exuberance in summer. An early morning walk in Coalpits Wash from July through September may result in finding only 12 to 15 bird species. Swallows and swifts, and an occasional Common Raven, hunt for food along the washes before the day becomes too warm and the desert animals find seclusion from the summer sun. The songs of House Finches may still be heard, as well as the sad calls of the Say's Phoebes. Black-throated Sparrows may still be found with a little searching, but most of the avian population that brightened the desert a few weeks before will have departed.

The RIPARIAN WOODLAND, too, is sparsely populated by birds in summer. Because July and August are not good birding months in Zion Canyon, Zion Park visitors often get the impression that southern Utah is a poor place for birds. However, the riparian woodland along the Virgin River and at the Springdale ponds still contain a few lowland species.

A visit here during early mornings may result in finding 25 to 35 kinds of birds, a few of which may not be found anywhere else within the Zion Park area. Typical summering birds of this river valley include the American Kestrel, Mourning Dove, Black-chinned Hummingbird, Ash-throated Flycatcher, Western Kingbird, swallows, Bewick's and House Wrens, Phainopepla, Warbling Vireo, Lucy's Warbler, Yellow-breasted Chat, Black-headed and Blue Grosbeaks, Lazuli Bunting, Song Sparrow, Bullock's Oriole, House Finch, and Lesser Goldfinch.

By the late summer, the PINYON-JUNIPER WOODLAND contains only a shadow of its springtime bird population. Most of the nesters have moved onto the higher terraces; only a few remain in this dry woodland environment. The lower parts of the pinyon-juniper community are almost devoid of birds, while the upper parts contain a noticeably larger population. This is due to cooler temperatures and, rarely, a spring or stock pond. The most common birds summering here include the Mourning Dove, Hairy Woodpecker, Western Scrub-Jay, Plain Titmouse, Bewick's Wren, Blue-gray

Gnatcatcher, Solitary Vireo, Black-throated Gray Warbler, and Black-headed Grosbeak.

The HIGH COUNTRY is at its best in summer. The late snows and cooler climate offer more moisture and a later blooming season. The results are more tolerable temperatures and available food and water. Nesting may continue through much of the summer, and some late nesting birds may still be incubating in late July. On the other hand, some early migrants may already be deserting their high country breeding grounds to begin their southward journeys. And a few more northern species, such as male Rufous Hummingbirds, may already put in their appearance. Generally, the high country bird population probably peaks in mid-July; immature birds, as well as those that have moved onto the higher terraces from their breeding grounds in the canyons and lower terraces, are present.

A visit to the high country in summer may result in finding as many as 45 to 55 bird species in a day. The best localities for bird finding are in the vicinity of the Kolob Reservoir and Blue Springs Lake. Of special interest are such highland residents as the Blue Grouse, Band-tailed Pigeon, Red-naped Sapsucker, Brown Creeper, Yellow-rumped (Audubon's) Warbler, Red Crossbill, and Pine Siskin.

The WATER AREAS in Zion National Park and vicinity are good places to find birds in summer. Water is then at a premium, for once the seeps and smaller springs become dry, the river, streams, ponds, and lakes become the center of bird activity. Therefore, these localities offer the best overall bird finding during the summer months; to find birds from July through September you must visit this environment. If two full days are available for birding during your stay in Zion, one day should be spent in the Virgin River Valley, and the other day should be spent in the vicinity of the Kolob Reservoir and Blue Springs Lake. As many as 65 to 75 bird species may be found on such a two-day search.

The Winter Months

Winter does not really begin in Zion Park and vicinity until the first snow falls in October, November, or December. Although the high country is cold and bleak during midwinter, relatively mild temperatures may prevail in the low canyons and desert areas. Snow rarely lies on the ground in the lowlands for long, and daytime temperatures may reach the mid-40s (Fahrenheit) throughout much of the winter.

The DESERT offers the warmest environment during the winter months, although cold winds sometimes force birds to find shelter in protected side-canyons. Most abundant of the wintering birds in the lowlands are the Dark-eyed (Oregon) Juncos and White-crowned Sparrows. Large flocks of these ground-feeders are not uncommon along the washes and on the flats. Other wintering species to be expected in the desert include the Gambel's Quail, Greater Roadrunner, Say's Phoebe, Rock and Bewick's Wrens, Loggerhead Shrike, Spotted Towhee, Western Meadowlark, and House Finch.

The RIPARIAN WOODLAND is a relatively popular bird habitat during winter. The streamsides and open side-canyons, where the broadleaf vegetation comes in contact with the pinyon-juniper woodland, seems to be most popular. Typical wintering birds of the riparian woodland include the Hairy and Downy Woodpeckers, Northern (red-shafted) Flicker, Black-capped Chickadee, Bushtit, Ruby-crowned Kinglet, Western Bluebird, Townsend's Solitaire, Spotted Towhee, and Dark-eyed (both Oregon and Gray-headed) Junco.

The PINYON-JUNIPER WOODLAND supports all of the full-time resident birds in winter, such as the Western Scrub-Jay, Plain Titmouse, Bushtit, and Canyon and Bewick's Wrens; but winter-resident-only species are few and far between. Exceptions include those areas adjacent to the riparian woodland and open flats, where those birds may forage for food among the evergreens. And the open flats add to the wintering populations. Watch there for the Northern Harrier and flocks of Horned Larks and Mountain Bluebirds.

Very few birds can usually be found in the HIGH COUNTRY during the winter months. A day along the upper Kolob Terrace Road may result in finding only eight to 10 kinds of birds. Watch for the Red-tailed Hawk, Golden Eagle, Clark's Nutcracker, and Common Raven. But a visit to a stand of pine and fir in protected side-canyons, such as in upper Emerald Pool Canyon, however, may offer a somewhat larger number of high country species. Wintering birds utilizing the protected side-canyons may include the Steller's Jay, Mountain Chickadee, White-breasted Nuthatch, Red Crossbill, and Cassin's Finch. The Red-breasted Nuthatch and Evening Grosbeak may be added to this list some years; they appear sporadically, being common some years and completely absent other years.

The WATER AREAS in the lower portions of the Zion Park area offer fairly good birding in winter, although the highland areas are often frozen over from December through February. The more common winter visitors in the lowland waterways and ponds include the Pied-billed Grebe, Mallard, Northern Pintail, Common Merganser, American Coot, Belted Kingfisher, Black Phoebe, American Dipper, Song Sparrow, and Red-winged Blackbird. In addition, watch for Bald Eagles along the Virgin River; this species has increased considerably since the use of DDT was outlawed in the United States.

There is no better indicator of an area's winter bird populations than the annual CHRISTMAS BIRD COUNTS (CBCs). On one day each winter, within a two-week period around Christmas, CBC participants count all the birds they can find within one established 15-mile diameter circle. The Zion National Park circle, with its center at the West Temple, includes a portion of Zion Canyon and the Virgin River Valley to Virgin, Utah, and portions of the Kolob Terrace.

A grand total of 111 bird species have been tallied on 25 Zion CBSs from 1970 through 1994. However, only 21 species were detected on all 25 counts: Mallard, American Kestrel, Gambel's Quail, Belted Kingfisher, Red-naped Sapsucker, Downy and Hairy Woodpeckers, Northern Flicker, Western Scrub-Jay, Common Raven, Black-capped Chickadee, Canyon and Bewick's Wrens, Ruby-crowned Kinglet, American Robin, European Starling, Spotted Towhee, Song Sparrow, White-crowned Sparrow, Dark-eyed Junco, and House Sparrow. And an additional 22 species—Great Blue Heron, American Wigeon, Sharp-shinned and Red-tailed Hawks, Greater Roadrunner, Black and Say's Phoebes, Pinyon Jay, Mountain Chickadee, Plain Titmouse, Bushtit, Brown Creeper, Rock Wren, American Dipper, Golden-crowned Kinglet, Western Bluebird, Townsend's Solitaire, Yellow-rumped Warbler, Red-winged

Blackbird, House Finch, Lesser Goldfinch, and Pine Siskin—were missed only on one to five counts. Forty-four species were recorded only on one to five counts.

An average of 3,288 individuals of 69 species were detected on the 25 CBCs. A high of 6,524 individuals of 68 species were tallied in 1987, and a high of 76 species (5,624 individuals) were recorded in 1988. Low counts of 44 and 48 species were tallied in 1970 and 1971 by only two and four counters, respectively, but 20 to 38 counters participated in each CBC from 1984 to 1994.

The CBCs also provide reasonably good trend data on avian populations, both generically and specifically. For instance, numbers of certain wintering raptors—including the Bald Eagle; Sharp-shinned, Cooper's, and Red-tailed Hawks; and American Kestrel—have increased considerably during the last decade, which directly correlates with the 1972 ban of DDT use in the United States and Canada. Additional references to the Zion CBCs will be included in the annotated list of species.

The Annotated List
of Species

The following is an annotated list of 287 species of birds that has been reported for Zion National Park and vicinity. The majority of these—252—are included in the regular list of species that follows, but 35 are hypothetical and are included in a second list—Birds of Uncertain Occurrence—on pages . This second list includes all those that are not adequately documented by either a specimen or a photograph, or by five or more sight records from unimpeachable sources.

All common and scientific names used are those suggested by the American Ornithologists' Union's *Check-list of North American Birds*, sixth edition (1983), and supplements (1985, 1989, 1993, & 1996), hereafter referred to as the AOU Checklist. Also, I have attempted to identify pertinent observers when giving details of specific sightings; in some cases, however, full names are unknown.

The terms used to describe the status of the various birds are defined as follows:

Abundant	Can be found in sizable numbers (50+ per day), without any particular search, in the proper habitats at the right time of year.
Common	Can usually be found in moderate numbers (10–50 per day), in the proper habitats at the right time of year.
Fairly Common	Can usually be found in small numbers (5–10 per day), in the proper habitat at the right time of year.

Uncommon	Can usually be found in low numbers (1–5 per day), in the proper habitat at the right time of year.
Rare	Not expected, but 1 to 5 individuals occur annually.
Casual	Totally unexpected; only a few sightings each decade.
Sporadic	May be present in numbers some years, and totally absent other years.
Permanent Resident	A bird that remains in the area throughout the year and does not migrate.
Summer Resident	A non-permanent resident bird that breeds in the area; it may arrive as early as March and remain as late as October.
Post-nesting Visitor	A bird that visits the area in summer but does not breed there; one that wanders to the Zion Park area after nesting.
Migrant	A bird that passes through the area only in spring and/or fall, from March to June and/or late July to early November, sometimes lingering for a few days to a few weeks.
Winter Resident	A non-permanent bird that remains in the area all winter; it may arrive as early as September and remain as late as May.

Also, all locations mentioned in the text were derived from the *Zion National Park Utah* map (Zion Natural History Association 1994). And, because a few terms are mentioned numerous times, they will be abbreviated as follows:

AOU	American Ornithologists' Union
CBCs	Christmas Bird Counts
NPS	National Park Service
ZCVC	Zion Canyon Visitor Center
ZNP	Zion National Park

Birds of Regular Occurrence

Family Gaviidae: Loons

Common Loon. *Gavia immer.*
Rare spring and casual fall migrant.
This large, northern water bird occurs only on the larger reservoirs and ponds. Spring records extend from three individuals found on March 3, 1974, at the F. D. Gifford Pond in Springdale (Dane Gifford), to one at Blue Springs Lake on June 4, 1978 (Jerome Gifford). Spring reports also include two sightings in Springdale (three individuals on March 3, 1974, by Dane Gifford, and one on March 23, 1970, by Jerome Gifford) and five sightings at the Grafton Ponds, all by Jerome Gifford: one on March 28, 1985; two individuals on April 11, 1982; three on April 13, 1983 (also seen by Jewel Gifford); five on April 18, 1983 (also seen by Kirk Topham); and three on April 29, 1983. And there are two high country reports in spring, both from the Kolob Reservoir: Cathy Pasterezyk found one on May 16, 1982; and Terry Boykie discovered one there on May 20, 1984.

There are only three fall reports for the Zion Park area. The first record is one discovered by Dennis Carter at the Kolob Reservoir on September 5, 1962; Peter Scott found a dead bird at Springdale on November 2, 1975 (the specimen is part of the ZNP study collection); and Jerome Gifford reported a lone bird at the Grafton Ponds on November 24, 1983.

The Pacific Loon (*Gavia pacifica*) has also been recorded from southwestern Utah and should be expected in the Zion Park area: one that was found by Neal Stephens at Ivins Reservoir, St. George, remained from July 9–30, 1990 (Kingery 1990), and two were found at the Quail Creek Reservoir: Terry Sadler reported one on May 1, 1995, and Steve Summers found one on June 22, 1995.

Family Podicipedidae: Grebes

Pied-billed Grebe. *Podilymbus podiceps.*
Rare year-round resident; fairly common migrant and winter visitor.
The first area record is a lone bird with a Western Grebe on North Creek Pond on December 20, 1962 (Wauer). Since then, it has been

reported for area reservoirs and ponds every month, although it is present only at select ponds during the nesting season. In 1984 and 1985, Jerome Gifford found at least two nesting pairs at the Grafton Ponds, including one immature bird on July 22, 1984, and six fledglings on July 13 and 22, 1985.

Any further development of the Virgin River Valley at Springdale and below is likely to eliminate essential nesting habitat for this secretive water bird.

It is most numerous from early August, through the winter months, to early May when one or two individuals can usually be found at all the lowland ponds—occasionally it can be found in the high country (when open water exists) at the Kolob Reservoir and Blue Springs Lake. One or two individuals were tallied on seven of 15 Zion Canyon CBCs from 1970 through 1994: in December 1971, 1973, 1978, 1980, 1981, 1983, and 1994.

Horned Grebe. *Podiceps auritus.*
Casual migrant and winter visitor.

Fall records extend from an early sighting, on September 2, 1984, to several from October 3 to December 8, including 12 individuals on November 8, all from the Grafton Ponds by Jerome Gifford. In addition, Robert Tweit reported 14 on the Kolob Reservoir in "early October 1982" (NPS files), and I found four individuals there on October 8, 1995. It has been reported only twice in winter: Gifford recorded one at Grafton on December 26, 1984, and seven there on January 7, 1987.

Spring reports are limited to one individual at Grafton from March 1–21, 1985, and one in breeding plumage there from April 10–12, 1982, all by Gifford; he photographed the later bird on April 12.

Eared Grebe. *Podiceps nigricollis.*
Common migrant and uncommon winter visitor.

Records of this little grebe exist at area reservoirs and ponds year-round, although there is no evidence of nesting. Post-nesting and migrant birds may appear in early July and peak in mid- to late September; there are scattered reports from all elevations into early winter. The first area record was at Kolob Reservoir on September 5,

1962 (Dennis Carter). I found one at Blue Springs Lake on August 30, 1964; Jerome Gifford and Glen Arnold found four individuals at the Kolob Reservoir on September 27, 1973; I found five there on October 2, 1995; and Jerome Gifford recorded it at the Grafton Ponds almost daily from July 8 through October 1981.

The first winter record was a bird that remained at the Grafton Ponds from mid-December 1970 to January 22, 1971 (Gifford). Since then, up to 115 individuals (on January 17, 1987) have wintered there. On 25 years (1970–94) of CBCs, numbers have varied from none on 18 years, one to four on six years, to 95 individuals on December 27, 1993. Wintering birds, apparently, are sporadic in occurrence.

Spring migrants begin to move through the region by mid-March and reach a peak in late April (22 at Grafton on April 20, 1985, and 16 there on April 25, 1984); scattered reports continue to mid-June. Some of the Grafton winter birds remained until June 6 (Gifford in 1984). Gifford photographed three birds in breeding plumage at the North Creek Pond on May 9, 1976. Another individual was found on the highway in Springdale by Louise Arnold; it was photographed by Gifford and released in the Virgin River.

This grebe is undoubtedly more common than reported since most of the birds that breed in western North America leave the Great Salt Lake in their fall/winter migration and fly south, at night, on a course that would take them over the Zion Park area. On one such migration, they were downed by inclement weather and as many as 2,500 were found near Cedar City (Jehl 1993).

Western Grebe. *Aechmophorus occidentalis.*
Rare migrant.

Spring records of this large grebe extend from March 28 to April 25, all from the Grafton Ponds by Jerome Gifford, to one later report: Gifford found eight on the Kolob Reservoir on May 21, 1982. There are no further records until September 19, 1983 (one found by Kirk Topham at the Grafton Ponds), followed by several other Grafton sightings through October 19, 1984 (by Gifford). One individual was found at Blue Springs Lake on September 27, 1973, by Gifford and Glen Arnold, and four individuals were also found there on September 27, 1971 (Gifford). There also is a later sighting of two birds at Grafton by Jerome and Jewel Gifford on November 23, 1984. And there is a lone winter record; the first area sighting was one at the North Creek Pond on December 20, 1962 (Wauer).

The AOU split Western Grebes into two separate species in 1985: Western and Clark's Grebes. There are at least two area sightings of Clark's Grebe, earlier considered only a "light color phase" of the very similar Western Grebe. However, until the Clark's Grebe is further documented by a photograph or additional sightings, it will be considered hypothetical (p. 163).

FAMILY PELECANIDAE: PELICANS

American White Pelican. *Pelecanus erythrorhynchos.*
Casual migrant.

The first report of this huge water bird was one that landed in the East Fork of the Virgin River on November 15, 1934; it "injured itself badly on a gravel bar, and was roped by a local cattleman who happened to see the accident. It died soon, after which I examined and identified the skin" (Presnall 1935). The species was next reported below Rockville by Dale Dockstader on October 1, 1978. The third and fourth sightings were at the Grafton Ponds on October 17, 1983, and October 14, 1984, both by Jerome and Jewel Gifford; the 1983 bird was found dead on October 24. And on September 21, 1994, Raymond Mustoe reported two flocks of "about 50 each in two Vs, flying southeast." And there is one spring record; Rick Boretti reported that "close to 100 American White Pelicans flew overhead (observed from Deertrap Mt.). Flying in formation . . . east to west, over East Temple west over the Streaked Wall, Altar of Sacrifice area, west toward LaVerkin" (NPS files).

FAMILY PHALACROCORACIDAE: CORMORANTS

Double-crested Cormorant. *Phalacrocroax auritas.*
Rare spring migrant.

There are scattered reports from March 18 to May 18. The first record is one found by Glen Arnold and Scott Ashman at the F. D.

Gifford Pond in Springdale on April 16, 1975; it was photographed that same day by Jerome Gifford. Except for two birds found at the Grafton Ponds on March 28, 1983 (Jerome Gifford), all reports are of lone birds. And there is a lone summer report: Jewel Gifford found one at Rockville on July 24, 1987.

FAMILY ARDEIDAE: BITTERNS AND HERONS

Great Blue Heron. *Ardea herodias.*
Uncommon migrant and winter visitor; irregular summer visitor.
This large, long-legged wader has been recorded every month, although the fewest records occur from early May to mid-June. It, apparently, once nested in the riparian zones along the Virgin River; Russell Grater found a recently constructed nest in Parunuweap Canyon on October 9, 1940. There are only a handful of summer sightings: Jack Davis found one near the Zion Lodge on June 27, 1965, and Jerome Gifford recorded lone birds at the Grafton Ponds almost daily from mid-June to early August in 1983. By September it can be expected anywhere along the Virgin River, and numbers remain steady all winter to early March, after which it is less numerous. It also can be found in the high country in late summer and fall; I found tracks at Blue Springs Lake on August 20, 1964; Charles Torrance reported one at the Kolob Reservoir on September 5, 1980; and Clifford and Cathy Felix reported one there on September 11, 1993.

On 25 Zion National Park CBCs (1970–94), Great Blue Herons were recorded every year but 1972, with high counts of 10 in 1994 and nine in 1988 and 1989. High spring and fall numbers include five at the Grafton Ponds on April 22, 1984 (Kirk Topham), and eight there on July 13, 1987 (Topham and Jewel Gifford).

Great Egret. *Ardea albus.*
Casual migrant.
This tall, all-white wader has been recorded from April 9 (three in 1985 by Jerome Gifford) to June 5 (one in 1984 by Kirk Topham and Jewel Gifford) in spring, all from the Grafton Ponds, and only twice in the fall: Jerome Gifford found lone birds at Grafton on September 23 and October 16, 1981. There also is a single winter record: Shane

Great Blue Heron

Pruett reported one "flying away from Springdale on Jan. 26 [1995]. Saw about ten minutes later on . . . pond at Rockville" (NPS files). And there is an earlier specimen, taken by Andrew Barnum in nearby Washington on May 10, 1948, in the Dixie College collection.

Snowy Egret. *Egretta thula.*
Uncommon spring and rare fall migrant.

Records extend from March 1 to June 14 in spring and from August 23 to October 14 in fall; and there is a lone winter sighting: Kirk Topham and Jewel Gifford found two at the Grafton Ponds on December 10, 1990. The majority of the spring records range from April 10 through May; two earlier sightings and one later sighting include lone birds at the Springdale and Grafton Ponds on March 1 and March 21, 1983, respectively, and one at Grafton on June 14, 1985, all by Jerome Gifford. Except for eight individuals found near the Temple of Sinawava—with a lone Cattle Egret on May 18, 1975, by Dr. and Mrs. Otto Mackenson, three seen at a stock pond near the southwest corner of the park on May 29, 1965, by Clyde and Lois Harden, and the one December report—all records are of single birds. Interestingly, the first report of this bird was of one that "was blown to the ground near the east boundary during an unseasonable snowstorm in May, 1933, and identified by Gordon Croft" (Presnall 1935).

Cattle Egret. *Bubulcus ibis.*
Casual migrant; probably increasing.

The first report of this recent North American invader was of a single bird, apparently traveling with eight Snowy Egrets, found at the Temple of Sinawava by Dr. and Mrs. Otto Mackenson on May 18, 1975. That bird also was observed by J. L. Crawford and Peter Scott. The second Zion record was a lone bird found in a Springdale field by Betty and Frank Urban on November 28, 1981; it also was seen by James Fraley. And Kirk Topham next reported one at the Grafton Ponds on March 22, 1982.

Since then it has been reported irregularly between March 22 and mid-May in spring, and between September 20 and early December in fall and early winter; the latest report was one found by Kevin Wallace at Springdale on December 4, 1983. The highest number of birds was 24 at the Grafton Ponds on May 8, 1986 (Jerome Gifford).

Green Heron. *Butorides virescens.*
Casual migrant and post-nesting visitor.

The first record of this little heron was one found on the December 17, 1973, CBC; it has not been seen in winter since. The few existing spring and fall records extend from one seen by a park visitor (NPS files) below Coalpits Wash on March 3, 1981, to several during late April and May at the Grafton Ponds in spring (Jerome Gifford), and lone birds at the Grafton Ponds on August 29 and 30, and November 12, 1983 (Gifford). This bird nests in riparian habitats along Santa Clara Creek and near St. George (Wauer 1969), and so post-nesting visitors should be expected along the lowland waterways.

Black-crowned Night-Heron. *Nycticorax nycticorax.*
Irregular visitor.

Records of this nocturnal heron are widely scattered along the Virgin River. The first report is a specimen taken at Springdale by D. E. Beck on July 19, 1933 (Dixie College collection). It was next reported there on July 13, 1936, by E. H. Cantrell, Jr., and Jerome Gifford found one along the river at Springdale on December 4, 1967, and on December 26, 1969. Glen and Louise Arnold next found one at the Springdale Ponds on December 8, 1973; Jerome and Jewel Gifford found one at the Grafton Ponds on April 20, 1985; and Kirk Topham reported two there on July 13, 1987.

FAMILY THRESKIORNITHIDAE: IBISES AND SPOONBILLS

White-faced Ibis. *Plegadis chihi.*
Uncommon spring and rare fall migrant.

Records extend from March 24 to May 31 in spring, and from August 12 to October 9 in fall. The first report is a specimen taken at Springdale by Rollo Beck on May 4, 1935 (Dixie College collection). It was next reported at a pond below Coalpits Wash on April 23, 1965, by Clyde and Lois Harden and me. And on September 13,

1971, Ellen Strauss found one at the Kolob Reservoir. Since then it has been recorded irregularly along the Virgin River and at the Grafton Ponds. And there are two out-of-ordinary reports: Jonathan Moser found a lone bird flying over the Zion Narrows near Orderville Canyon on August 19, 1983, and Paul Bauer found a dead bird in the Virgin River; it had a wound in its neck that may have been caused by a predator such as a Peregrine Falcon. Although the majority of the sightings are of one to six birds, Kirk Topham found a high of 17 individuals at the Grafton Ponds on May 7, 1986.

FAMILY CICONIIDAE: STORKS

Wood Stork. *Mycteria americana.*
One record.
There is a lone specimen of this tropical stork—taken at Virgin on August 28, 1939, by W. S. Long (1940)—in the University of Utah collection.

FAMILY ANATIDAE: SWANS, GEESE, AND DUCKS

Tundra Swan. *Cygnus columbianus.*
One record.
There is a single specimen in the Dixie College collection; it was collected at Springdale by A. F. Bruhn in February 1949. Additional records can be expected with the increasing number of area reservoirs. Steve Hedges found three at St. George during the winter of 1994–95.

Snow Goose. *Chen caerulescens.*
Rare migrant.
Spring migrants have been recorded in the Zion Park area from February 15 (four individuals found at Springdale by Louise Arnold and Austin Excell in 1973) to April 3, when William Fisher discovered a flock of 23 birds flying down Zion Canyon in 1965. The earliest park record was six birds flying up Zion Canyon on March 6, 1964 (Bruce Moorhead). Fall migrants do not reach southwestern Utah until early November; area records range only from November 6 to

December 7, although Jerome Gifford reported that one Snow Goose spent the winter of 1986–87 with a flock of domestic geese at Mooney's Pond in Rockville.

All but one of the Snow Goose records represent typical white birds, but Jerome Gifford found an "immature blue morph Snow Goose at the Grafton sewage ponds from 27 Nov. to 7 Dec. 1983" (Gifford 1987). This blue-phased bird was once considered a separate species. And the very similar Ross' Goose (*Chen rossii*), once lumped with the Snow Goose, should be looked for; this smaller, stubby-billed goose winters irregularly in the St. George area.

Canada Goose. *Branta canadensis.*
Rare migrant; uncommon winter resident; probable nester.

Records of this familiar goose, which has a black head and neck and white throat-patch, exist in the Zion Park area every month but May and June. And two adults and two juveniles, found below Rockville by Leon Lewis on July 6, 1974, may represent local nesting. Another summer record is of a lone bird found floating down the Virgin River along the Narrows Trail on July 17, 1991, by Frank Hays.

It is most common during the winter months, especially since the Grafton Ponds were completed. In 1981–82, Jerome Gifford recorded it almost daily at Grafton from December 1 to February 13. And in 1984–85, he recorded it almost daily there from August 6 to the end of February; only a few were present in December, the numbers increased to 27 and 65 individuals during the first half of February, then sharply declined by the end of the month. The highest number recorded was 150 individuals on the river between Springdale and Rockville on February 20, 1985 (Jerome Gifford).

Wood Duck. *Aix sponsa.*
Uncommon migrant and winter visitor.

There are records for every month but June and August; Jerome Gifford observed it almost daily at the Grafton Ponds from September 17, 1982, through the winter, to April 5, 1983, and from September 25, 1983, to May 2, 1984. The earliest park record is of four or more birds seen repeatedly at the Springdale Ponds by Dennis Carter and Dick Russell during February and March 1964. During the winter of 1975–76, Jerome Gifford found up to 10 individuals there. And there

Green-winged Teal

also is a record at Birch Creek in Zion Canyon on December 10, 1975 (Lynn Ballard). Jerome Gifford's midsummer record is of a male in eclipse plumage at Grafton from July 10–18, 1981.

Green-winged Teal. *Anas crecca.*
Rare summer resident; common migrant; fairly common winter resident.

Dennis Carter and I found a pair of birds on a small pond near Lava Point on June 3, 1964; I found two pairs at a pond on Little Creek on May 27, 1965, and again on June 8; Clyde Harden found young birds at this same location on June 21, 1965.

Post-nesting birds reach the Zion lowlands by early August and usually remain through the winter months to as late as the end of May. Jerome Gifford found it almost daily at the Grafton Ponds from August 15, 1981, to April 28, 1982; October 5, 1982, to May 15, 1983; August 29, 1984, to May 25, 1985; August 18, 1985, to May 20, 1986; and August 31, 1986, to March 31, 1987. The maximum number recorded was 70, 60, and 86 individuals on March 4 and 19, and May 2, 1986, respectively (Jerome Gifford). And on 25 CBCs (1970–94) it was recorded 18 times, including a high of 33 individuals on December 27, 1984.

Mallard. *Anas platyrhynchos.*
Common permanent resident.

Although it is present year-round at ponds in the lowlands, high-country birds move to lower elevations during severe winter periods. Nesting occurs wherever habitat exists: Jerome Gifford found 30 to 50 fledglings at the Grafton Ponds annually from 1981 to 1987, and five adults and seven young were found at Blue Springs Lake on August 30, 1964 (Wauer).

There also is an increase in the number of Mallards at high-country ponds and lakes by midsummer, which is the result of post-nesting birds as well as migrants. Steve and Priscilla Summers reported 20 birds at the Kolob Reservoir on August 14, 1995, and I counted more than 50 individuals there on October 2, 1995. High Mallard counts in the lowlands include 218 at Grafton on November 24, 1983, and 400 to 450 there on January 20–29, 1984, by Jerome Gifford.

Northern Pintail. *Anas acuta.*
Fairly common migrant and uncommon winter visitor.

Records exist within the Zion Park area year-round, although the handfull of summer reports are probably non-nesting vagrants: three birds at Blue Springs Lake all during late May and June in 1965 (Harden, Lueck, and Wauer), and two July sightings at the Grafton Ponds on July 3 and 21, 1983, by Jerome Gifford.

Fall migrants may appear at lowland ponds by August 11, a few can be expected to remain throughout the winter months, and the latest of the spring migrants have been reported to May 21. A high count of 44 individuals was reported at Grafton on February 15, 1986 (Jerome Gifford). And Pintails were recorded on 10 of 25 CBCs (1970–94), with a high of 35 birds on December 27, 1983.

Blue-winged Teal. *Anas discors.*
Uncommon spring migrant; casual summer vagrant; rare winter visitor.

Spring records extend from March 6 to May 7, with a high of 56 birds at the Grafton Ponds on May 2, 1982 (Jerome Gifford); there is a later movement through the area from June 14 to 25. In 1985, a non-nesting pair remained at the Springdale Ponds until June 24; there are no reports for July, but Gifford reported it at Grafton twice in August, on August 5 and 26, 1983. There are no reports for September, October, or November, but there are a few scattered sightings in December and January. And it was recorded on only one of the 25 CBCs (1970–94): one individual on December 26, 1970.

Cinnamon Teal. *Anas cyanoptera.*
Fairly common summer resident in the high country; common migrant at all elevations; casual winter visitor.

The first and only nesting record is of five individuals found at a pond along the drainage below Kolob Reservoir on May 12, 1965, and a nest found among the tules there on May 27 (Wauer). But there are scattered reports in both the highlands and lowlands all summer, especially at the Grafton Ponds.

Fall migrants appear in August: Jerome Gifford reported migrants at Grafton from August 14 to October 6, 1983; August 16 to October 14, 1984; and August 13 to October 15, 1985. I found 12 individuals at the Kolob Reservoir on October 2, 1995. An occasional bird will remain in the area during November, December, and January, and spring migrants appear in early February. Gifford reported finding northbound birds at Grafton from February 19 to May 2, 1983; February 9 to May 20, 1984; February 8 to May 10, 1985; and February 12 to May 21, 1986. He recorded a high of 50 birds on February 17, 1984, and 40 on April 3, 1983, and March 26 and 30, 1984.

Northern Shoveler. *Anas clypeata.*
Uncommon migrant and winter visitor.

Records extend from September 27 to May 18. Although Jerome Gifford recorded one or two individuals at the Grafton Ponds on September 26 and November 18 and 30, 1985, it is most common from early to late November and from mid-January to late April, including sightings in Parunuweap Canyon and Blue Springs Lake. Gifford reported a high count of 10 females and one male at the Grafton Ponds on May 18, 1985. It was recorded on only four of 25 CBCs (1970–94): nine on December 26, 1970, three on December 19, 1972, three on December 27, 1983, and one on December 28, 1987.

Gadwall. *Anas strepera.*
Uncommon migrant and winter visitor.

Records extend from October 1, through the winter months, to May 11; and there also are four reports at the Grafton Ponds in summer: Jerome Gifford found it there on July 29 and August 5, 12, and 14, 1983. It is most numerous in spring from early March to mid-April; Gifford reported a high of 14 individuals at Grafton on April 17, 1984. And it was recorded on nine of 25 CBCs (1970–94): one on December 19, 1972 and December 27, 1990; four on December 27, 1983, December 27, 1991, and December 27, 1994; two on December 27, 1985, December 29, 1986, and December 27, 1989; and three on December 28, 1992.

American Wigeon. *Anas americana.*
Fairly common migrant and winter visitor.

Records, all from the lowlands, extend from September 8, through the winter months, to May 7. Jerome Gifford recorded the species at the Grafton Ponds from October 16, 1981, to April 3, 1982; September 23, 1982, to March 28, 1983; October 17, 1983, to March 30, 1984; October 15, 1984, to April 23, 1985; and October 5, 1986, to February 14, 1987. He reported a high of 46 birds at Grafton on January 11, 1981.

There also are seven reports of male Eurasian Wigeons (*Anas penelope*) from the Lava Hills Golf Course at St. George: March 18, 1982; February 2 and December 13 and 23, 1983; and January 24, November 29, and December 26, 1984. This species should be looked for at the Grafton and Springdale Ponds.

Canvasback. *Aythya valisineria.*
Uncommon migrant and winter visitor.

Records, all from the lowlands, extend from September 2, through the winter months, to April 28—except for sightings at Blue Springs Lake: one on February 19, 1983, and four on October 20, 1971 (Jerome Gifford). Gifford found it most consistently at the Grafton Ponds between early November to mid-March, including a high of 11 birds at the Springdale Pond on November 18, 1971. Christmas Bird Count participants found it on only five occasions in 25 years (1970–94).

Redhead. *Aythya americana.*
Fairly common migrant and rare winter visitor.

There are reports every month but June, and it is most numerous in spring from February to early April. Jerome Gifford found the species almost daily at the Grafton Ponds from August 1 to November 10, 1982; November 13, 1983, to May 16, 1984; and from November 9, 1984, to April 3, 1985. He reported a high count of 13 birds at Grafton on March 13, 1984. This diving duck was also recorded on six of the 25 CBCs (1970–94): 1973, 1974, 1976, 1983, 1990, and 1994.

Ring-necked Duck. *Aythya collaris.*
Common migrant and fairly common winter visitor.

Zion area records extend from September 11, through the winter months, to April 26. And there is a lone summer sighting at the Grafton Ponds on July 11, 1982 (Jerome Gifford). During four seasons, Gifford recorded Ring-necked Ducks at Grafton almost daily from September 29, 1981, to April 19, 1982; October 11, 1982, to April 6, 1983; October 1, 1983, to April 24, 1984; October 3, 1984, to April 3, 1985; and from October 10, 1985, to April 5, 1986. High counts during this period included 218 on December 13, 1986, 294 on December 25, 1986, 300 on December 30, 1984, and 256 on February 11, 1985. It also was recorded on 19 of 25 CBCs (1970–94).

Lesser Scaup. *Aythya affinis.*
Fairly common migrant and winter visitor.

Records extend from September 25, through the winter months, to April 22, from ponds and lakes in both the high country and lowlands. Jerome Gifford reported it from the Grafton Ponds almost daily from October 9, 1982, to April 22, 1983; October 25, 1983, to April 17, 1984; October 15, 1984, to March 30, 1985; and from November 13, 1985, to April 16, 1986. Gifford found a high of 13 birds at Grafton on November 14, 1986. Christmas Bird Count participants recorded it on nine of the 25 years (1970–94).

Oldsquaw. *Clangula hyemalis.*
One record.

A lone female in winter plumage appeared at the Grafton Ponds on November 20, 1983, and it remained until December 2 (Jerome and

Jewel Gifford). It was photographed by Jerome Gifford on November 25 and 26, and the record and photograph were later published in *American Birds* (Kingery 1984). Although this northern duck is considered a "rare transient of northern Utah" (Hayward et al. 1976), this was the first record for southern Utah.

Surf Scoter. *Melanitta perspicillata.*
Casual fall/early winter visitor.

There are three records only, all from the Grafton Ponds. A female first appeared on November 30, 1981, and remained until December 14 (Jerome Gifford and Kirk Topham). Another female appeared there on November 20–27, 1985 (Gifford and Topham), and Gifford discovered a male there on October 4 and 5, 1986. These were the first records for southern Utah.

White-winged Scoter. *Melanitta fusca.*
Casual fall visitor.

There are three records, the first two occurring within a two-week period: a female was first observed at the Grafton Ponds on October 25–27, 1984, by Jerome and Jewel Gifford; it was photographed by Jerome on October 26. Then on October 26, four females appeared (Jerome Gifford); two and three individuals remained until November 6. They were seen on October 27 by the Giffords and Ella and Richard Sorenson; and two of these birds were photographed by Jerome on October 31. The third record was of two immature females on October 19, 1986 (Jerome Gifford); one female left the next day, but the other remained until October 22. Like the Surf Scoter, these were the first records for southern Utah.

Common Goldeneye. *Bucephala clangula.*
Fairly common migrant and uncommon winter visitor.

Records extend from October 7 (male seen at the Springdale Ponds by Wauer, Sheri Fedorchak, and others in 1995) to May 11. Jerome Gifford recorded this species at the Grafton Ponds from January 27 to March 30, 1983; November 16, 1984, to May 1, 1985; November 20, 1985, to March 20, 1986; and from November 26, 1986, to March 2, 1987. He recorded a high of 49 individuals at Grafton on

February 17, 1985. In addition, it was recorded on only seven of 25 CBCs (1970–94).

Bufflehead. *Bucephala albeola.*
Uncommon migrant and winter visitor.

Records, all from the lowlands, extend from October 2, through the winter months, to April 26; there also is a May 16, 1982, report at Grafton by Jerome Gifford. During four seasons, Gifford recorded this duck almost daily at the Grafton Ponds from November 1, 1981, to March 30, 1982; October 2, 1982, to April 5, 1983; October 25, 1983, to April 26, 1984; and from November 31, 1984, to March 30, 1985. The highest number recorded during this period was five males and 18 females on November 23, 1982. It also was found on five of 25 CBCs (1970–94).

Hooded Merganser. *Lophodytes cucullatus.*
Casual migrant and winter visitor.

The earliest record of this little water bird in the Zion Park area was a female collected on the Virgin River by R. H. Cantrell, Jr., in November 1936. It was not seen again until 1967, when Jerome Gifford found four on the river in Springdale on December 13 and 26. Since then it has been reported sporadically, including a high of seven individuals at the mouth of Zion Canyon on January 13, 1977, and a male in breeding plumage at Grafton on October 30, 1982 (Gifford).

Common Merganser. *Mergus merganser.*
Casual summer resident; fairly common migrant and winter visitor.

Ward Gibson was the first to find it nesting in Zion Canyon in spring 1973; Peter Scott observed a female with a single youngster at the mouth of Parunuweap Canyon on July 10; and Louise Arnold and Jerome Gifford observed seven and eight birds in eclipse plumage at the Temple of Sinawava on August 31. And in 1974, nesting birds were discovered on both forks of the Virgin River (Peter Scott).

It is most numerous as a migrant and winter visitor. Jerome Gifford recorded birds at the Grafton Ponds from November 23, 1978, to March 5, 1979; November 24, 1982, to March 30, 1983;

November 22, 1984, to March 18, 1985; and November 13, 1986, to March 2, 1987. And it was found on 19 of 25 CBCs (1970–94), with a high count of 29 individuals on December 27, 1983.

Red-breasted Merganser. *Mergus serrator.*
Uncommon migrant and casual winter and summer visitor.
Records exist for every month but February and September. Spring migrants are most numerous from March 12 to May 21; there are a scattering of reports from June 10 to August 13, and another scattering from October 26 to January 3. High counts include 78 at Grafton on November 23, 1984, and 88 there on March 28, 1985, both by Jerome Gifford. This species was not recorded on any of the 25 CBCs from 1970 through 1994.

Ruddy Duck. *Oxyura jamaicensis.*
Uncommon migrant and winter visitor.
Records of this little duck extend from July 22, through the fall and winter months, to May 22; there are no June reports. Jerome Gifford recorded it almost daily during five seasons: from August 28, 1981, to May 22, 1982; September 30, 1982, to May 1, 1983; August 28, 1983, to May 13, 1984; August 31, 1984, to April 27, 1985; and from September 30, 1985, to May 17, 1986. It also was recorded on 10 of 25 CBCs (1970–94), including high counts of 20 birds on December 27, 1983, and again on December 27, 1994. Although the majority of the Zion Park area sightings are from the lowlands, it also has been reported for the high country: 12 were found on the Kolob Reservoir and one was found on Blue Springs Lake October 31, 1963 (Wauer and Dennis Carter); and one was reported for the Kolob Reservoir on January 8, 1972 (Gifford and Peter Scott).

Family Cathartidae: American Vultures

Turkey Vulture. *Cathartes aura.*
Common summer resident and uncommon migrant.
This large scavenger has been recorded as early as March 1 and as late as October 30, and there also are two December reports: David Excell and Lance Gifford found three in Coalpits Wash on December 19,

1974, and Jerome Gifford found one at Birch Creek in Zion Canyon on December 27, 1971.

Nesting has been recorded on several occasions. Clifford Presnall (1935) was first to report nesting birds: "In 1934 a nest on the slopes of Mount Majestic was noted by many who traveled the West Rim Trail, especially after the young ones started slowly learning to fly on June 10." In 1964, Nelson Maloney found a juvenile bird, which was not able to fly, at Virgin in early June; Jerome Gifford recorded juveniles at Rockville on May 30, 1967, at Springdale and Rockville on May 2 and 30, 1985, and at Grafton on April 24 and 26 and May 7, 1986.

Migrants begin to move through the area by the last of March, increase in number during April and the first half of May, and then numbers trickle off to mid-June. These birds, as well as the summer residents, can be expected at all elevations and occasionally can be found in numbers: Shane Pruett found a "kettle of 20 with one osprey" (NPS files) over Rockville on March 22, 1994; I found 23 at Coalpits Wash on April 11, 1963; and Rudy Lueck discovered 55 in the vicinity of a dead horse near Lava Point on September 14, 1964. Most sightings, however, are of one to five individuals. The fall migration is barely noticeable, as the majority of the high country birds do not drop into the canyons but continue south over the upper terraces.

FAMILY ACCIPITRIDAE:
OSPREY, EAGLES, HAWKS, AND ALLIES

Osprey. *Pandion haliaetus.*
Rare spring and casual fall migrant.

Spring records extend from March 22 to May 24, and there are two June sightings: Tom Gillette reported an "adult at Narrows at mouth of Kolob Creek" (NPS files) on June 8, 1991, and Don and Martha Shearer found one at the Kolob Reservoir on June 21, 1993. There are no records from June 22 until September 4, when Tom Gillette found one soaring over Blue Springs Lake in 1994. There are four additional reports in September, one in October (Frank Loskot observed one near the Grotto Picnic Area in Zion Canyon on October 24, 1993), and Jerome Gifford observed one at the Grafton

Ponds on December 30, 1984. There are no other winter reports until March 22.

Bald Eagle. *Haliaeetus leucocephalus.*
Uncommon winter resident and casual visitor at other times.

The majority of sightings extend from mid-November to mid-February, but it has been recorded all times of the year and at all elevations. There is no positive evidence of nesting, although Jerome Gifford observed two individuals—one of which was carrying a long string of fibers that may have been nesting materials—at the Clear Creek Ranch (along the North Fork Road) on May 22, 1960.

Wintering birds are most likely to be found in the Zion Park area near the East Entrance and along the Virgin River from Zion Canyon to Virgin. Midwinter raptor surveys, conducted by Larry Hays of the NPS, covering these areas from 1980 through 1988, revealed that more Bald and Golden Eagles utilize the open slopes east of the East Entrance than anywhere else. There also are a few winter sightings in Zion Canyon: one at the Court of the Patriarchs on December 11, 1971; another near Cascade Spring on December 19, 1971; one at Weeping Rock on January 8, 1972 (all by Gifford), and one in upper Zion Canyon on January 14, 1977, by Wayne Hamilton. In addition, Bald Eagles were recorded on 17 of 25 CBCs (1970–94).

Although most Bald Eagle observations are of one or two individuals, five were recorded on the December 27, 1993, CBC; Liesl Schindler reported five sitting in a large ponderosa pine at the East Entrance on January 3, 1984; and Victor Willis found three Bald Eagles soaring over the Kolob Reservoir on September 29, 1994. Wintering Bald Eagles are most numerous along Route 9 between the East Entrance and Mt. Carmel Junction and in the open valleys west of the park. Congregations of 100 or more birds have been reported near Cedar City on several occasions (Steve Hedges).

Northern Harrier. *Circus cyaneus.*
Uncommon migrant and winter visitor, and casual in summer.

It is most numerous from mid-November, through the winter months, to mid-March, typically soaring low over open fields in search of prey. Jerome Gifford found it almost daily in the Springdale/Grafton area from November 30, 1973, to March 31, 1974, and from December 10, 1984, to March 19, 1985. And CBC participants recorded it on 16 of 25 years (1970–94), with a high count of seven individuals on December 27, 1990.

Spring migrants pass through the area from mid-March to early May. And there are three summer sightings, although there is no evidence of nesting: I found one in Taylor Creek on June 20, 1963; Jerome Gifford found a male at Clear Creek Ranch on July 26, 1981, and a female there on August 23, 1981. Fall migrants normally reach the park area by the first week of September.

Sharp-shinned Hawk. *Accipiter striatus.*
Uncommon summer resident; fairly common migrant and winter resident.

This little accipiter is most numerous in the highlands in summer and the lowlands in winter, generally near populations of small birds on which it preys. Some birds may be permanent residents. Nesting occurs in the high country and at protected pine-fir niches in the canyons. I found a nest on a white fir at the base of Lava Point in early June 1963, and another nest with two young at Hepworth Wash on June 28, 1966; Peter Scott reported a pair nesting on a Douglas fir in Emerald Pools Canyon in 1974, and a pair in a white fir grove in Taylor Creek in May 1975; Scott Nichols reported a nest with two adults and "two one-week-old babies" (NPS files) in Birch Creek on June 9, 1983; and Shane Pruett discovered a nest in Clear Creek on June 8, 1994.

It is most evident during migration from mid-March through April in spring, and from early September to mid-November in the fall. And it can be found consistently all during the winter months: Jerome Gifford recorded it almost daily at Springdale, Rockville, or Grafton from early November through mid-March during the 1980s; it also was recorded on all but two of 25 CBCs between 1970 and 1994, with an average of three individuals and high counts of six individuals on December 27, 1990, and December 27, 1994.

Cooper's Hawk. *Accipiter cooperii.*
Common year-round resident and migrant.

Like its smaller cousin above, this accipiter is more numerous in the high country in summer and in the lowlands in winter. There are several nesting records; it probably is the park's most common raptor,

Cooper's Hawk

although Red-tailed Hawks are seen more often because of their soaring habits. Jerome Gifford found a nest on an ash tree along North Creek on May 23, 1961, and I located three nests in 1965: on a box elder in the Court of the Patriarchs on May 6, one containing two eggs on a Douglas fir in upper Emerald Pools Canyon on May 18, and one on an aspen at the top of Carpenter Hill on June 9. More recently, the park staff has made a concerted effort to monitor nesting Cooper's Hawks, and two dozen or more nests have been located in riparian vegetation along the Virgin River and several side-canyons; the nests have also been found in mixed forest vegetation at higher elevations in canyons and on the higher terraces of the plateau. For instance, in 1974, Ken Kertell and Peter Scott found five active nests on the Kolob Terrace; these nests produced 16 fledglings.

Cooper's Hawks are most evident during migration, when they occur at all elevations. Although most of the summer residents and migrants move out of the area, a few remain in the lowlands all winter. On 25 CBCs (1970–94), it was recorded 17 times, with a high of eight individuals on December 27, 1994.

Northern Goshawk. *Accipiter gentilis.*
Rare permanent resident.

This powerful accipiter has been recorded year-round in the Zion Park area, but there is no evidence of nesting. I did find a pair in the Bridge Mountain area on May 3, 1963; Kurt Ranslem reported a young bird "about four miles south of Kolob Reservoir" (NPS files) on August 3, 1974; and there are several reports from Lava Point from June 10 to September 12. Birds may appear anywhere in the area; there are scattered records at all elevations, from Coalpits Wash (Jerome Gifford on February 26, 1976), to the center of Springdale (Gifford found one harassing an American Kestrel there on December 22, 1981), to one found over Oak Creek Canyon on September 22, 1995 (Wauer), to those found on the Kolob Terrace. And it was recorded on four of 25 CBCs (1970–94), in 1978, 1981, 1991, and 1994.

This bird may be more common than records indicate. U.S. Forest Service surveys in the Dixie National Forest, directly north of ZNP, produced 18 active nests, including two near the Kolob Reservoir in 1995, according to Priscilla Summers.

Common Black-Hawk. *Buteogallus anthracinus.*
Casual early summer visitor.

This Southwestern hawk once nested in the riparian vegetation along the Virgin River between Springdale and Grafton, but, due to the considerable development in this area, it is extremely unlikely that it will return. The best chance of finding this bird in the Zion Park area is in early spring, when one may be searching for an adequate nesting site, or in midsummer when a post-nesting visitor from less developed sites may appear; it still nests in Utah in Beaver Dam Wash, in the extreme southwestern corner of the state (Kate Grandison).

It was first recorded in the Zion Park area, as well as in the state of Utah on May 4, 1962, when Dennis Carter found one at Springdale. A pair was seen again on May 24, and nesting was suspected but not confirmed. In 1963, two Black-Hawks were seen by Carter on April 9, I photographed those birds on April 18, and Carter located a nest in a cottonwood south of Springdale on May 13 (Carter and Wauer 1965). An injured or sick bird, found at Berry Spring on April 21, 1966, was collected (Wauer) and represents the first specimen for the state (Wauer 1969; Wauer and Russell 1967). A second Utah nest was discovered at Springdale in 1971 by Jerome Gifford, who later summarized its status and described its habitat and behavior in a comprehensive article for *Utah Birds* (1985). Although an occasional Black-Hawk was seen in Springdale until 1976, and others at Grafton in 1981 and 1985 (Gifford), there have been no additional area reports.

Swainson's Hawk. *Buteo swainsoni.*
Rare summer visitor and casual migrant.

There are fewer than a dozen reports during the last 20 years, although it was listed by both Clifford Presnall (1935) and Russell Grater (1947) as a "common" and "uncommon" summer resident in ZNP. By the 1960s, it was considered a "rare" summer resident in the high country" (Wauer and Carter 1965), based on only four observations: lone birds were recorded near Potato Hollow on July 25, 1963, and near Kolob Reservoir on May 27, June 1, and June 26, 1965 (Wauer). Since then, it has been recorded only six times: Jerome Gifford reported a late migrant at Springdale on December 11, 1971, a dark phased bird at Springdale on October 12, 1973, one at the Springdale Ponds on November 27, 1973, and one at the mouth of Zion Canyon on November 17, 1981; Tasha MacIlreen reported one over Deertrap Mountain on October 16, 1994; and Don Morris found one soaring over the Watchman Area on August 17, 1995.

Red-tailed Hawk. *Buteo jamaicensis.*
Common permanent resident and migrant.

This is the most often seen raptor in the Zion Park area, often found perched on snags or cliffs along the lower canyons or upper terraces or soaring overhead. Winter raptor surveys, conducted in the Virgin River drainage by David and Margaret Mindell (1980) in 1979–80, revealed that Red-tails "accounted for 38% of the observations" of all raptors found.

There are several nesting records for all elevations: I found a nest on a ponderosa pine along the Kolob Terrace Road at 7,900 feet elevation on June 27, 1963; Bruce Moorhead and I found a nest, containing a juvenile bird, on a ponderosa pine on Deertrap Mountain on June 21, 1965; Clyde and Lois Harden found a nest, also containing a juvenile bird, near Home Valley Knoll on June 22, 1965; Clarence Todd reported nests near Rockville in the summer of 1973 and in July 1975; Ken Kertell and Peter Scott found a nest on a cliff at the mouth of Zion Canyon in the summer of 1975; Jerome Gifford found birds barely able to fly at Grafton on July 9, 1981; and Nancy Fonicello found a nest in Imlay Canyon on August 9, 1992.

Migrants are barely noticeable, although fall migrants pass over certain high country localities, such as Kolob Reservoir and Lava Point, in numbers, and they apparently move beyond the Zion Park area for the winter. The wintering birds appear to be the same individuals that are present year-round. The species was missed only once in 25 years of CBCs (1970–94), with high counts of 12 on December 27, 1985, and 11 on December 29, 1986, and December 27, 1993.

Ferruginous Hawk. *Buteo regalis.*
Casual summer and winter visitor and migrant.

There are only a handful of reports in the Zion Park area, although it is a reasonably common nesting bird on the sagebrush-pinyon-juniper flats west of the Kolob Canyons in Iron County (Staats 1995). I found lone birds over North Creek on June 1, 1965, near Maloney Hill on October 31, 1965, near the East Entrance on

November 7, 1965, at Taylor Creek on November 29 and December 5, 1965, and over Springdale on April 25, 1966; Peter Scott (1975) recorded one "migrating with Red-tails" near the Kolob Reservoir on September 12, 1974; Jerome Gifford found one at Coalpits Wash on April 2, 1978; David and Margaret Mindell found it on their 1979–80 wintering raptor surveys only at Washington on January 31, and at Hurricane on March 8; and Tim Manns reported one near the South Entrance on the 1991 CBC.

Rough-legged Hawk. *Buteo lagopus.*
Uncommon migrant and fairly common winter visitor.

Records extend from August 30 to May 2, and there are three later reports: I found two individuals near the Kolob Reservoir on May 27, 1965, and one at the same location on June 1; and Jerome Gifford observed one soaring over Springdale on June 23, 1974. Other reports of migrants include lone birds at the mouth of Zion Canyon on April 10, 1973, at the East Entrance on September 24, 1978, over Rockville on March 11 and 14, 1982, and at Kolob Reservoir on October 14, 1983, all by Gifford.

This northern hawk probably is sporadic in occurrence; Gifford recorded it only once during the winter of 1970–71, none in the winters of 1971–72 and 1972–73, 13 times in 1973–74, 10 in 1974–75, five in 1975–76, three in 1976–77, seven in 1977–78, 19 in 1978–79, eight in 1979–80, seven in 1980–81, two in 1981–82, and 18 times in 1982–83. A high count of nine individuals, "circling" below a Bald Eagle near Virgin, was reported by M. Hilkey on January 1, 1984. And it was recorded on eight of 25 CBCs from 1970 to 1994.

Golden Eagle. *Aquila chrysaetos.*
Fairly common permanent resident.

Soaring birds can usually be found, with patience, year-round over Zion Canyon and elsewhere in the park area. Courtship and nesting begins very early in the year. David and Margaret Mindell reported courtship flights near the East Entrance on February 14, 1980, and Rick Boretti located three nests in 1993: one 1,673 feet high on a cliff in Steven's Canyon on March 30, one with two young in Hop Valley on April 14, and one in Dennett Canyon on May 31. And I photographed a fledgling, barely able to fly, in Zion Canyon in late June 1962.

Golden Eagle

The Golden Eagle is one of Zion Park's most representative birds, and it appears that the park population has remained high in spite of being persecuted outside the boundary. Although most reports are of one or two birds, I found four circling over the West Temple on January 9, 1965; Jerome Gifford observed three together on the Lower Kolob Terrace on December 27, 1971; and Scott and Janice Staats reported five over North Creek on January 22, 1995. In addition, Frank Cope and Jill Blumenthal watched a Red-tail "mobbing" an immature Golden Eagle over the East Rim Trail on September 9, 1986 (NPS files), and on February 2, 1994, Steve King reported two Golden Eagles circling for 10 minutes over a newborn bighorn before flying away.

FAMILY FALCONIDAE: CARACARAS AND FALCONS

American Kestrel. *Falco sparverius.*
Common summer and winter resident; fairly common migrant.
This attractive little falcon can be found in the Zion Park area year-round, and some individuals are permanent residents. Nesting occurs

American Kestrel

on cliffs and in cavities on large trees at all elevations. Jerome Gifford found a pair nesting in an old church at Grafton in mid-May 1979; they produced three youngsters. More recently, Jeff Kamps found a nest, containing two nestlings, in a cavity in a ponderosa pine near Checkerboard Mesa on July 17, 1995.

The permanent population is augmented during fall and winter by migrants and wintering birds from the north. On September 29, 1971, Gifford recorded a high count of 23 Kestrels in a half-mile stretch of roadway on the "Big Plains" south of Rockville. Peter Scott (1975) reported that "in fall, from 20 to 30 migrating Kestrels may sometimes be seen along the Kolob Reservoir [Terrace] Road." David and Margaret Mindell found it second in numbers only to Red-tailed Hawks on their winter raptor surveys in 1980–81. And on 25 CBCs from 1970 to 1994, it was never missed; participants found an average of 11 individuals, a low of three birds on December 26, 1970, and a high count of 20 on December 27, 1983.

Although this little falcon is best known for preying on insects and small rodents, I found one attempting to capture bats at Springdale on March 29, 1965; it made five passes without success.

Merlin. *Falco columbarius.*
Casual winter visitor.

Records exist every month, but it normally can be found in the Zion Park area only from early October, through the winter months, to mid-March. However, a pair of these little northern falcons uncharacteristically spent almost five years in Springdale from September 9, 1972, through 1977 (Jerome Gifford and others); there was never an indication of nesting. During 25 years of CBCs (1970–94) it was recorded only three times: one individual on December 18, 1976, and December 27, 1990; and three birds were tallied on December 27, 1994.

Peregrine Falcon. *Falco peregrinus.*
Uncommon permanent resident.

This is a characteristic bird of Zion's abundant canyons and high cliffs, and NPS biologists monitored a total of 13 active territories in 1995; at least 29 fledglings were produced from eleven eyries, according to David Sinton (1995). This is a far cry from the low numbers recorded in the 1950s and 1960s, before DDT was outlawed in the United States and Canada in 1972. Thereafter, Peregrine recovery programs were established at a number of Rocky Mountain sites, and the birds began an amazing recovery. Today, the ZNP population represents one of the highest in the state, and perhaps one of the densest in the United States, according to Clayton M. White.

Peregrines are most often seen during the breeding season, which begins in late February or early March, when courting birds are more easily detected by their loud cries and constant activity near their eyries. Egg-laying occurs from late March to mid-May, hatching takes place in 32–34 days, and fledglings normally can be found in another 45–47 days. Common prey species during the breeding season varies with locality, but, on the greater Colorado Plateau, Shirley Teresa (1989) found remains of White-throated Swifts and Violet-green Swallows in 98% of the nests examined; jays and shorebirds in 60% and 67% of the nests, respectively; various waterfowl

Peregrine Falcon

were found in 43% of the nests; Mourning Doves in 21% of the nests; and smaller songbird remains were found in only a few nests.

Teresa (1989) also analyzed habitat requirements for nesting Peregrines in ZNP. She found that cliff heights averaged 2,090 feet, that the eyrie site averaged 1,975 feet high and 230 feet from the cliff-top, and that the distance to the nearest riparian habitat was 49 to 2,904 feet, with an average of 1,168 feet. The NPS closes key nesting sites to rock climbers between February 1 and the end of July.

Where is a visitor most likely to find a Peregrine during the breeding season? The upper portion of Zion Canyon, from the Grotto Picnic Area to the Great White Throne parking area, is best. During the remainder of the year, anywhere along Zion Canyon and elsewhere in the park is possible for sharp-eyed observers.

Prairie Falcon. *Falco mexicanus.*
Rare permanent resident.

Although this falcon can appear almost anywhere in the Zion Park area, it prefers open sagebrush habitats at mid-elevations. Nesting has been recorded in Cave Valley and along the south wall of the West Temple (Wauer), and Rick Boretti found a nest on Beatty Point on May 26, 1993. There is probably a nesting territory in Coalpits Wash, as well, because of the number of sightings reported there from late December to early June. It is less numerous on the higher terraces; the only high country report is one at Blue Springs Lake on September 6, 1974, by Peter Scott. It was recorded on only three of 25 CBCs (1970–94): lone birds were recorded in 1977, 1978, and 1988.

FAMILY PHASIANIDAE: GROUSE, TURKEY, AND QUAIL

Ring-necked Pheasant. *Phasianus colchicus.*
Uncommon permanent resident.

This long-tailed exotic was first introduced into the Zion Park area by the Utah Fish and Game Department in the 1940s, but the earliest report was in Springdale on November 12, 1960 (Jerome Gifford). Gifford next found lone males at Springdale on March 17 and 29, 1964, and McDowell discovered a nest with eight eggs in the Watchman Orchards on April 13, 1964; the nest was later deserted. Since then, Ring-necked Pheasants have been found in

Zion Canyon at least up to the Zion Lodge. However, the overall population may have peaked and leveled off; Gifford, in listing all of his observations, year-by-year from 1971 to 1984, revealed increased annual sightings from 10 to 97 individuals between 1971 and 1976; afterward their numbers gradually declined and then began fluctuating: from 51 to 36 then from 8, 7, 13, 11, 8, to 5 between 1977 and 1984. Christmas Bird Count totals for 25 years (1970–94) also reflect a decline, with high counts of 16 and 11 on December 31, 1975, and December 18, 1976, respectively, and five to none (except for 9 in 1994) from 1977 to 1994.

Pheasant populations have declined significantly throughout all of southwestern Utah in the last 20 years. This has been the result of urban development and changes in agricultural practices, according to Steve Hedges. .

Blue Grouse. *Dendragapus obscurus.*
Fairly common permanent resident.

This elusive bird is reported most often from high country areas such as the Kolob Reservoir, Lava Point, Potato Hollow, West Rim, and the East Entrance, for example, a hen with two chicks were reported at Lava Point on July 30, 1993 (Lars Boll). However, it also visits the lower canyons on occasion: Doyle Winder found one at the South Entrance in 1969; Kathy Heyder reported one at the ZCVC on October 26, 1973; Jerome Gifford found one in Springdale on November 24, 1979; and one found by Doyle Winder in Springdale on December 22, 1981, spent more than a month (until January 30, 1982) in town, roosting in the shrubbery at the home of Myrna Fraley. This was the only year this species was recorded on the local CBC.

Wild Turkey. *Meleagris gallopavo.*
Rare permanent resident.

Although Turkey feathers have been found in association with Indian ruins in Parunuweap Canyon, there were no historical records for the Zion Park area. The first known report is a lone bird at Blue Springs Lake on August 30, 1964, and June 1, 1965 (Wauer). I later learned of a private introduction in the high country at about that time, and, according to Fred Bryant and Darrell

Blue Grouse

Nish (1975), additional southwestern Utah transplants occurred in 1968 and 1972–73. The next report was of six individuals found on the East Rim, July 12, 1967, by Jerome Gifford and Earl and Margaret Grant. And on August 16, 1970, a female was observed one mile north of the Pine Creek junction in Zion Canyon (Gifford). Then a female, perhaps the same bird, was seen several times between the Zion Lodge and Grotto Picnic Area in January, and Doyle Winder released a male Wild Turkey nearby. They were seen frequently in this vicinity through April, and eventually a female (probably the same bird) laid eggs in a nest along the Riverside Walk; it was later abandoned, according to Richard A. Stuart (NPS files).

Reports of Wild Turkeys in the high country—from Pine Valley, Indian Hollow, West Rim, Lava Point, Wildcat Canyon, and Blue Springs—continued, including a flock of 50 at Indian Hollow on October 29, 1972 (Lewis Beatty). More recently, Keith Sherman reported one on the West Rim on January 11, 1991; Jon Nelson found six there on December 25, 1992; Ivan Kassovic reported one at the Temple of Sinawava on May 1, 1993; Laird Naylor found a hen with two chicks in Echo Canyon on June 26, 1993; James Van Sickel found "about 80" at Firepit Knoll on January 12, 1994; Jerry Davis and Dan Habig reported a "large group of various ages" (NPS files) there on February 6; and Rupert Pilkington reported flocks of 20 and 39 there on February 8; and, finally, Betty and I surprised a covey of about 15 individuals of various ages along the North Fork Road on October 6, 1995.

Gambel's Quail. *Callipepla gambelii.*
Fairly common permanent resident.

This bird occurs only in the lowlands; it has been reported most often in Coalpits Wash, lower Parunuweap Canyon, and along the Virgin River between Virgin and the mouth of Zion Canyon. Jerome Gifford found a female with eleven chicks in Oak Creek Canyon on July 6, 1951, another covey of 12 birds in Springdale on June 11, 1953, two adults with three juveniles at the Springdale Ponds on August 24, 1975, and six adults with three chicks on June 25, 1977.

Quail populations are usually cyclic in nature, depending upon the weather and available food, predators, and habitat changes. But it appears that this species has generally held its own reasonably well over the last 25 years. Christmas Bird Count numbers from 1970 through 1994 have remained high, with an average of 42 individuals tallied annually, a low of two birds on December 27, 1984, and a high count of 117 birds on December 28, 1991.

FAMILY RALLIDAE: RAILS, GALLINULES, AND COOTS

Virginia Rail. *Rallus limicola.*
Rare summer and winter resident.

Suitable habitat for this rail is scarce in the Zion Park area, and the few ponds where this bird was recorded regularly during the 1970s and 1980s have largely been destroyed or degraded in favor of new motels and other businesses. However, prior to then, Jerome Gifford recorded it year-round at the Springdale Ponds, including high counts of five on January 12, 1976, seven on October 29, 1978, six on September 9, 1979, seven on January 8, 1980, six on December 17, 1980, and five on October 18, 1981. And it was recorded on 15 of 25

CBCs (1970–94). There also is a sighting of a lone bird at Watercress Spring on the Riverside Walk on December 5, 1971 (Gifford). Although there is no evidence of nesting at those ponds, it most surely occurs; I collected a downy black juvenile at Washington on October 19, 1965 (Wauer 1969).

Sora. *Porzana carolina.*
Rare summer resident and winter visitor.
As in the case of the larger Virginia Rail, essential habitat is scarce for this rail. However, this bird has been recorded at the Springdale Ponds year-round, and Steve and Priscilla Summers also found four birds below the Kolob Reservoir on August 14, 1995. Jerome Gifford found one or two individuals present in Springdale during a breeding bird census from April 23 to July 10, 1976, and also during a winter bird population study from December 17, 1976, to February 4, 1977. In addition, Soras were recorded on eight of 25 CBCs between 1970 and 1994.

American Coot. *Fulica americana.*
Rare summer resident; fairly common migrant; common
winter visitor.
This water bird is an opportunist that nests in almost any available habitat. Although it was not recorded prior to 1960, when the Springdale Ponds were dredged, it has been seen almost every year since. Jerome Gifford collected a specimen at a stock pond on Smith Mesa on June 26, 1960. I found two birds at the Springdale Ponds all winter and spring 1964–65, and one several times at the North Creek Pond during May, June, and July 1965. And Gifford found the first nest, containing four eggs, at the Jesse Gifford Pond in Springdale on June 20, 1971. In 1972, three pairs raised eight young there; one nest was found in 1973, four nests in 1975, and one in 1975 (Gifford). It probably also nests in the high country at Blue Springs Lake and Kolob Reservoir; Don and Martha Shearer reported a pair at Blue Springs Lake on June 21, 1993.

Migrants reach the Zion Park area by early September. Gifford recorded arrival and departure dates during five seasons at Springdale: November 18, 1971, to July 18, 1972; September 9, 1972, to July 1, 1973; November 3, 1973, to May 12, 1974; October 2, 1974, to July 6, 1975; and September 28, 1975, to May 3, 1976. And in 1983, he found the species at the Grafton Ponds on July 5; they remained year-round, including 100 birds from November 22 to April 25, 1984, and a maximum of 136 Coots on February 3. Christmas Bird Count participants recorded birds on 19 of 25 years (1970–94), with high counts of 125 on December 27, 1983, and 168 on December 27, 1994.

FAMILY CHARADIIDAE: PLOVERS

Snowy Plover. *Charadrius alexandrinus.*
Four records.

The first sighting of this little shorebird for the Zion Park area was a lone bird at the Grafton Ponds on April 3, 1983 (Jerome Gifford). A second (assumably) Snowy Plover appeared at the Grafton Ponds on April 30, 1983, where it was photographed by Gifford and also seen by Jewel Gifford and Roy Given. And on March 28 and 29, 1985, another individual was found and photographed there by Gifford. In addition, Judy Perkins reported one along the North Fork of the Virgin River on August 16, 1991.

Semipalmated Plover. *Charadrius semipalmatus.*
Casual migrant.

Spring records range from April 21 to May 6, all from the Grafton Ponds, and include 18 birds that arrived on April 25, 1984, then gradually moved on, with the last individual leaving on May 6 (Jerome Gifford). Fall records extend from August 10 to October 27, including the earliest report of one at the Kolob Reservoir in "fall" 1975 and a second there on September 9, 1976 (Ken Kertell; NPS files). The highest fall count included four at Grafton on September 22, 1981 (Kirk Topham).

Killdeer. *Charadrius vociferus.*
Common summer resident and uncommon in winter.

This plover can be found at water areas and/or about cultivated fields year-round. Clifford Presnall (1935) first reported nesting pairs on Shunes Creek and in Coalpits Wash in 1934; and I found the species present in flooded fields near Blue Springs Lake in May and June, and a nest there on June 1, 1965. Jerome Gifford reported nesting in the lowlands in 1981: an adult with two very young chicks were at the Grafton Ponds on May 23; three adults and two juveniles were there on June 7; and a nest, containing four eggs, was at Grafton on June 21; hatched young were photographed on June 22. The highest number found at Grafton was 26 individuals on April 14, 1983 (Gifford).

Wintering Killdeers are not as reliable, but almost always can be found with patience. On 25 CBCs (1970–94), it was recorded on only eight years.

Mountain Plover. *Charadrius montana.*
One record.

A lone bird was found in a field about five miles below Rockville on April 11, 1965, by C. R. Skelton, who reported it to me. I collected and prepared it as a study skin for the Zion Park collection. The specimen represented only the second for Utah (Wauer and Russell 1967), although the first nesting records for Utah were recently recorded (Day 1994).

FAMILY RECURVIROSTRIDAE: STILTS AND AVOCETS

Black-necked Stilt. *Himantopus mexicanus.*
Uncommon spring and casual fall migrant.

Spring records extend from March 25 to June 1, and fall records range from August 24 to September 19. All the reports are from the Grafton Ponds, with eight exceptions: the earliest sighting was of a lone bird at a pond west of Coalpits Wash on May 6, 1964 (Dennis Carter and Dick Russell); and I found one at a pond along the North Fork Road on May 12, 1965, and another in Zion Canyon the following day. Peter Scott reported 20 Stilts at Blue Springs Lake on June 4, 1974, and he found six at the Kolob Reservoir on June 28, 1976; M. Callister reported eight at Blue Springs Lake on May 5, 1985, and Janet Ellis found 11 there on June 10, 1985; and Jennifer Gillette reported seven at Blue Springs Lake on June 1, 1994.

American Avocet. *Recurvirostra americana.*
Uncommon spring and rare fall migrant.

Spring records extend from a report of 11 birds at the North Creek Pond from March 15 to June 9, 1964 (Dennis Carter, Rudy Lueck, and Bruce Moorhead). Jerome Gifford recorded spring migrants at the Grafton Ponds from March 17 to May 16, 1983, and March 30 to May 2, 1985, with a high count of 80 on March 17, 1982.

Fall records extend from August 21 to September 30 (one seen at the Kolob Reservoir by Seth Phalen in 1974), including a high of 33 birds at Grafton on August 24, 1982 (Jerome and Jewel Gifford and Kirk Topham). And there is a lone October report (Gifford found one at Grafton on October 19, 1983) and two for November, both by Jerome Gifford: a flock of 20 individuals on the Virgin River at Rockville on November 3, 1974, and a lone bird along the East Fork on November 20, 1983.

FAMILY SCOLOPACIDAE:
SANDPIPERS, PHALAROPES, AND ALLIES

Greater Yellowlegs. *Tringa melanoleuca.*
Uncommon spring migrant.

Spring records by Jerome Gifford and Kirk Topham extend from March 17 to May 2, primarily at the Grafton Ponds. Except for eight individuals on March 30, 1984, and five on April 11, 1983, all other observations are of lone birds. There also are two later reports: Ken Kertell found a lone bird (probably a post-nesting vagrant) at the Kolob Reservoir on August 10, 1974, and Jerome Gifford found a very late migrant at Grafton on November 12, 1981.

Lesser Yellowlegs. *Tringa flavipes.*
Rare spring and casual fall migrant.

Spring records extend from March 19 to May 3, all from the Grafton Ponds by Jerome Gifford, with one exception: I collected a lone bird at the Springdale Ponds on April 29, 1965. A high count of 10 birds were photographed by Gifford on April 20, 1982. And there are four fall records: Ken Kertell found two birds at the Kolob Reservoir on August 23, 1974; and Gifford reported two at Grafton on August 8 and 29, 1981, and one there on August 24, 1982.

Solitary Sandpiper. *Tringa solitaria.*
Rare spring and fall migrant.

Spring records range from April 25 to May 18, all from the lowlands, and include a specimen collected at the Springdale Ponds on
April 29, 1965 (Wauer), and one netted and banded there on May 8,
1965 (Hardens and Wauer). Fall records extend from August 9 to
October 13, all from the Grafton Ponds, with three exceptions: lone
birds were found at the Kolob Reservoir on August 21 and 23, 1974,
by Seth Phalen and Ken Kertell, respectively; and Richard A. Stuart
reported one there on October 13, 1970.

Willet. *Catoptrophorus semipalmatus.*
Uncommon spring migrant.

Spring records, mostly from the Grafton and Springdale Ponds by
Jerome Gifford and Kirk Topham, extend from March 30 to May
13. Exceptions include 14 individuals in Coalpits Wash on April 11,
1973 (Joyce and Seth Phalen), and one found in the roadway at the
Temple of Sinawava by Tim Tibbitts and Larry Hays on April 25,
1984. The high count was 22 Willets at Grafton on April 24, 1981
(Topham). And there is also a report of a lone bird at Grafton on
July 21, 1983 (Gifford), presumably an early southbound migrant.

Wandering Tattler. *Heteroscelus incanus.*
One record.

A lone bird visited the Grafton Ponds from September 2 to 9, 1981;
it was seen by Jerome Gifford and Kirk Topham and photographed
on September 3 by Gifford. The photograph, later published in
American Birds (Kingery 1982), represents the first verified record for
the Zion Park area and only the third for Utah.

Spotted Sandpiper. *Actitis macularia.*
Fairly common summer resident and migrant; casual in winter.

This little sandpiper arrives in the Zion Park area as early as April 15,
and nesting birds may remain on their territories to mid-August. It
nests along the rivers and streams and at ponds at all elevations; six pairs
were present at Blue Springs Lake in June 1965; I found a nest, containing four eggs, on June 9. I also found a young bird along the Virgin
River above the Riverside Walk on May 25, 1965. And Jerome Gifford
found a nest along the river above Birch Creek on June 19, 1951.

Spotted Sandpiper

Fall migrants reach the lowlands in early September and some may linger into December and January; Gifford found birds still present at the Grafton Ponds on January 8, 1984. The highest number recorded was 28 at Grafton in April and 10 at the Kolob Reservoir in May (Gifford). Christmas Bird Count participants recorded this shorebird only three times (1978, 1980, and 1983) in 25 years (1970–94).

Marbled Godwit. *Limosa fedoa.*
Casual spring migrant.
Records range only from April 3 to 26. The first one was discovered at the Grafton Ponds by Kirk Topham on April 20, 1982; it was photographed that same day by Jerome Gifford. The same or another bird was found the next day, and three individuals appeared there on April 22 (Gifford and Topham). It was next reported at Grafton from April 2 to 26, 1983 (Gifford), and again from April 21–26, 1984 (Gifford). There are fall reports (July 22 to September 10) from the Cedar City area, so this bird should be expected in the Zion Park area at that time of year as well.

Sanderling. *Calidris alba.*
Casual spring migrant.

There are five reports, all by Jerome Gifford at the Grafton Ponds. One was first recorded on April 21, 1982; four individuals were found there on April 29, 1983; three and five birds were found there on April 29 and 30, 1984, respectively; and one was observed there by Jerome and Jewel Gifford on April 19, 1985.

Western Sandpiper. *Calidris mauri.*
Common spring and fall migrant.

Spring records extend from March 20 to May 11, including a high of 65 individuals at the Grafton Ponds on April 30, 1983 (Jerome Gifford). The latest spring report is a lone bird in Zion Canyon on May 11, 1965 (Wauer). And except for one found at a pond along the North Fork Road on May 2, 1964 (Wauer), all the spring reports are from the lowlands. Fall records extend from July 23 to October 5, mostly from the Grafton Ponds by Gifford; but Seth Phalen reported 12 at the Kolob Reservoir on August 23, 1974, and Peter Scott found one there on September 4, 1974. Fall observations included a high count of 21 individuals at Grafton on August 12, 1981 (Gifford).

Least Sandpiper. *Calidris minutilla.*
Fairly common spring and uncommon fall migrant.

Spring records, all from the lowlands, extend from March 19 to May 28, with the majority of sightings from April 12 to May 1 and a high count of 21 individuals on April 15, 1984 (Jerome Gifford). Fall records begin in the high country with 13 and 12 birds found by Ken Kertell at the Kolob Reservoir on July 16 and August 10, 1974, respectively, to a November 16, 1981 report at Grafton (Gifford). The bulk of the fall reports range between mid-August and mid-September and rarely exceed four birds at any time.

Baird's Sandpiper. *Calidris bairdii.*
Casual spring and fall migrant.

The first record of this shorebird for the Zion Park area was that of a lone bird found by Richard A. Stuart at the Kolob Reservoir on August 18, 1971. Four birds were reported there by canoeists on September 4, 1974, and seven individuals were found there on September

25 (Seth Phalen and Peter Scott). It was next recorded by Jerome Gifford at the Grafton Ponds on August 21 and 22, 1981, and on March 19 and April 17, 1982.

Pectoral Sandpiper. *Calidris melanotos.*
Casual spring and fall migrant.
Richard A. Stuart recorded one at the Kolob Reservoir on August 7, 1970, and another one there on August 26, 1971. It was next reported and photographed by Jerome Gifford at the Grafton Ponds on August 15, 1981. He reported three later observations, all at Grafton: September 12, 1981, March 19, 1982, and March 23, 1983.

Long-billed Dowitcher. *Limnodromus scolopaceus.*
Uncommon spring migrant.
Spring records, all from the lowlands, extend from March 14 to May 13, with the majority of these from mid-March to late April; a high count of 21 individuals was recorded by Jerome Gifford on April 25, 1984. There also is a single fall report: Gifford found two at Grafton on August 10, 1981.

Common Snipe. *Gallinago gallinago.*
Uncommon migrant and winter resident.
This shy, long-billed bird has been recorded in the Zion Park area lowlands year-round, although there are only two reports from May 25 to July 30: Jerome Gifford found lone birds at the Springdale Ponds on June 11, 1953, and on June 30, 1971. Fall migrants can be expected by the end of July, and winter birds normally arrive from mid-October to mid-November. Gifford recorded arrival and departure dates at Springdale and Grafton for several years as follows: November 17, 1971, to March 17, 1972; November 21, 1974, to May 19, 1975; November 27, 1975, to March 28, 1976; and November 26, 1981, to April 22, 1982. Wintering Snipe were recorded on 16 of 25 CBCs (1970–94), with high counts of six individuals on December 16, 1974, and December 18, 1976, and eight on December 27, 1980. Spring migrants can usually be detected by early March and until the end of April, and there are scattered reports until May 24.

Wilson's Phalarope. *Phalaropus tricolor.*
Uncommon spring and rare fall migrant; casual in winter.

Spring migrants are most numerous from late April to the end of May, and there is a later report of one at Springdale on June 4, 1974 (Jerome Gifford). Fall migrants have been recorded as early as July 30; Ken Kertell reported two from the Kolob Reservoir in 1974 and eight there on August 3; and Seth Phalen and Peter Scott found five at the Kolob Reservoir on September 4, 1974. Gifford reported the species at the Grafton Ponds from July 30 to August 15, 1981, including a high of 106 birds on August 10. There are a few scattered reports at Grafton from mid-September through the winter months, including an all-time high count of 138 birds on November 23, 1984 (Gifford), but it was not recorded on any of the 25 CBCs (1970–94).

Red-necked Phalarope. *Phalaropus lobatus.*
Casual spring and fall migrant.

The earliest record for the Zion Park area are two specimens (Dixie College collection) taken at Springdale on August 15, 1936 (Olive Brooks), and April 26, 1939 (R. Hafen). The next record is two birds found at Kolob Reservoir by Ken Kertell on May 12, 1974; a second one, in breeding plumage, was found there by Peter Scott on June 4. Then in 1981, Jerome Gifford found six at the Grafton Ponds on May 6, and lone birds on September 13 and 14 (also seen by Kirk Topham) and on October 13 and 14. Gifford reported four observations in 1982: a flock of 60 individuals appeared at Grafton on May 6; and three, eight, six, and two birds were found there on September 12, 13, 15, and 17, respectively.

FAMILY LARIDAE: GULLS AND TERNS

Franklin's Gull. *Larus pipixcan.*
Casual spring migrant.

Records range only from April 3 to April 30. The first reports included one found at the Grafton Ponds on April 21, 1982 (Kirk Topham and Jerome Gifford), and two found at Grafton on April 3 and one on April 11, 1983 (Gifford); and three were observed there on April 30, 1983, by Jerome and Jewel Gifford and Roy Given. There are two earlier specimens from outside the area: Ross Hardy and H. G. Higgins collected one from a flock of 20 birds at St. George on April 23, 1940, and I collected one of three birds found at Washington on April 15, 1966 (Wauer 1969).

Bonaparte's Gull. *Larus philadelphia.*
Four records.

The first report is one discovered by Ken Kertell at the Kolob Reservoir on October 20, 1975. Four birds were next photographed by Jerome Gifford at the Grafton Ponds on April 18, 1981; M. M. Simmons reported two at "Zion" (NPS files) on May 24, 1981; and Gifford photographed a lone bird at Grafton on April 10, 1982.

Ring-billed Gull. *Larus delawarensis.*
Uncommon spring and rare fall migrant; casual in winter.

Spring records extend from mid-February to May 11, and the earliest fall report is October 31; all records are from the Grafton Ponds. In 1983, Jerome Gifford recorded one to 64 individuals at Grafton continuously from February 25 through May 11. And in 1985, he found eight to 16 birds there from February 17 through March 30. However, in 1984, he found birds at Grafton as early as January 3, and one to 26 individuals were present there until May 7. A high count of 138 was recorded at Grafton on November 23, 1984 (Gifford).

California Gull. *Larus californicus.*
Uncommon spring and rare fall migrant.

Spring records extend from February 9 to May 17 in the lowlands, and there are three reports from the high country: I found three individuals above Blue Springs Lake on June 1, 1965; Richard A. Stuart reported one there on March 15, 1971; and Peter Scott recorded eight birds at Blue Springs Lake and five at the Kolob Reservoir on June 4, 1974. Jerome Gifford reported one to four birds at the Grafton Ponds from February 9 to April 7, 1982, and one to five individuals at Grafton from February 16 to April 4, 1983. A high count of 117 individuals were recorded on March 28, 1985 (Gifford).

Fall records include three birds at the Kolob Reservoir on August 21, 1974 (Seth Phalen), none in September, two reports on

November 9, 1982 (29 at Springdale and Grafton by Meridy Cross and Jerome Gifford), and two in December: one at Grafton on December 8, 1982, and one there on December 18, 1984 (Gifford).

Forster's Tern. *Sterna forsteri.*
Rare spring migrant and casual in summer and fall.

Spring records extend from April 18 to June 4, including a high of seven individuals at the Kolob Reservoir on May 12, 1974 (Ken Kertell). Clyde and Lois Harden reported birds at the Kolob Reservoir all summer 1967, Richard A. Stuart reported "small flocks of strays" (NPS files) at Springdale on June 27, 1971, and there are two August reports at the Kolob Reservoir: Seth Phelan found one there on August 21, 1974, and Mark Zolink and Riley Nelson reported one with a lone Black Tern on August 13, 1981.

FAMILY COLUMBIDAE: PIGEONS AND DOVES

Rock Dove. *Columba livia.*
Uncommon visitor.

This domestic, but feral, pigeon resides in the lower Virgin River Valley year-round, but it only occasionally is seen in the Zion Park area. It has been recorded on seven of 25 CBCs (1970–94), with high counts of 34 birds in 1993 and 1994.

Band-tailed Pigeon. *Columba fasciata.*
Fairly common summer resident.

There are numerous records in the high country from mid-May to early September; there are only scattered reports at other times of the year. The oddest of these is 50 to 100 birds found along Interstate 15—between Pintura and Black Ridge near the Kolob section of the park—on February 5, 1979, by Sheldon Olson. And there are three October reports: Eric Haskell found one below Potato Hollow on October 2, 1994; Jerome Gifford, J. L. Crawford and Hugh Kingery found four along the North Fork Road on October 20, 1973; and Gifford observed two on Carpenter Hill on October 27, 1973.

This large, native pigeon nests in the high country in early summer; it is most often reported from ponderosa pine areas, such as

Band-tailed Pigeon

Carpenter Hill, as well as at Lava Point and Potato Hollow. By mid-summer, flocks usually congregate at oak groves to feed on ripe acorns; Rudy Lueck reported a high of 50 to 75 birds at Carpenter Hill on August 4, 1959. And occasionally in midsummer they appear in and around Springdale and Rockville to feed on ripe mulberries and other fruit. Gifford reported up to 32 individuals at Springdale between June 3 and July 10, 1981, and one to 31 individuals there between May 19 and July 30, 1982. And on September 6, 1981, Gifford found several individuals in the Watchman Campground: "a cold front moved through on September 5, dropping two inches of rain and the low [temperature] on the 6th was 52 degrees F" (Gifford 1987).

White-winged Dove. *Zenaida asiatica.*
One record.

On April 23, 1984, Dane Gifford discovered a lone White-winged Dove at the Driftwood Lodge in Springdale. It remained there until April 27, during which time it was also observed by Jerome and Jewel Gifford, Catherine Matthews, J. R. Murphy, Louise Excell, and Kirk Topham; Jerome Gifford photographed it on April 27. While this is only one record, it certainly is not an unexpected species, considering its distribution in Utah (Behle et al. 1985).

Mourning Dove. *Zanaida macroura.*
Common summer resident; fairly common migrant; rare in winter.

It is most numerous from early April through September; Jerome Gifford recorded it almost daily during eight seasons at Springdale: from April 1 to May 27, 1972; April 30 to September 24, 1973; March 30 to July 5, 1974; April 5 to September 24, 1975; April 11 to October 7, 1976; April 10 to September 14, 1978; April 3 to August 14, 1979; and April 22 to September 27, 1980. It usually occurs in small flocks of eight to 25, but a flock of 34 appeared at the ZCVC during a snowstorm on May 5, 1964 (Dennis Carter). Gifford recorded higher counts of 58 at Springdale on April 26, 1975, 100-plus at Springdale on August 27, 1973, and 120 on the Big Plains south of Rockville on September 15, 1973.

The first nesting record is of a nest, containing two eggs, found on a small bush at the Springdale Ponds on June 8, 1965 (Wauer). Gifford found a nest with two eggs in Cave Valley, May 25, 1980; and he recorded it on breeding bird censuses at Coalpits Wash, Grafton, Springdale, Watchman Campground, upper Pine Canyon, East Entrance, and Lava Point.

Winter records are rather sparse; it was recorded on eight of 25 CBCs (1970–94), including a high count of 30 on December 31, 1975.

FAMILY CUCULIDAE: CUCKOOS AND ROADRUNNERS

Yellow-billed Cuckoo. *Coccyzus americanus.*
Rare summer resident and migrant.

Records extend from June 9 to October 12, and all are from the riparian woodlands in the lowlands. This is one of the park's latest summer residents to arrive. Although there is no evidence of nesting, its presence among the riparian vegetation all summer suggests it does nest in late June, July, or August. Increased reports from August 3 to September 26 may represent fledglings.

Greater Roadrunner. *Geococcyx californianus.*
Uncommon permanent resident.

Although this easily recognized cuckoo of cartoon fame can not be found anywhere with certainty, it is most often reported in the desert, from Coalpits Wash to Springdale, and occasionally in the vicinity of the South Entrance and the ZCVC. It also has been reported at higher elevations near the East Entrance and along the lower portion of the Kolob Terrace Road. And it has been recorded on 22 of 25 CBCs (1970–94), including a high count of five individuals on December 27, 1989. Although there are no records of nesting, it undoubtedly does nest in the lowlands.

FAMILY TYTONIDAE: BARN OWLS

Barn Owl. *Tyto alba.*
Casual permanent resident.

There are fewer than a dozen reports from various elevations. It was first recorded by Clifford Presnall (1935), who claimed that Vasco Tanner had "noted it in Zion Canyon during the fall and winter." Russell Grater next found one at Weeping Rock on July 14, 1971. It has since been reported from the Canyon Overlook Trail on August 9, 1973 (Glen Arnold); in the roadway near the little tunnel on September 23, 1973 (Glen Arnold and Dane and Jerome Gifford); near the East Entrance on December 26, 1975 and January 18, 1976 (Jerome Gifford); one was found dead on the Big Plains south of Rockville on November 3, 1978 (Dane Gifford); at Springdale on August 23, 1979 (Charles Torrance); and at Rockville on October 9, 1979 (Patsy Graves and Jeff Gubler). It was recorded on only one (3 on December 29, 1986) of 25 CBCs (1970–94).

FAMILY STRIGIDAE: TYPICAL OWLS

Flammulated Owl. *Otus flammeolus.*
Rare summer resident and sporadic migrant.

Records of this little, brown-eyed owl extend from May 7 to October 28. This bird was not known for the Zion Park area before I captured one in a mist net in Oak Creek Canyon on May 8, 1964; it was banded, photographed, and released. Another was found perched on a willow in the Watchman Residential Area the same day; it also was banded and released. Still another was found dead in Zion Canyon on May 11 (Frank Oberhansley); the specimen was preserved. These records, all obtained during a period of unseasonably cold, stormy weather, were some of the earliest evidence of migration (Wauer 1966). An additional Flammulated Owl was caught in a mist net at the Springdale Ponds on May 7, 1965 (Wauer, Hardens, and Dick Russell), one year after the first records and during a similar period of inclement weather; it too was banded, photographed, and released.

Although there are no actual nesting records, one found on a Douglas fir along the south fork of Taylor Creek, May 21, 1964 (Wauer), and an immature bird, too young to fly, found in the Watchman Campground on August 21, 1974, suggests nesting. Jerome Gifford photographed this later bird that died, and Peter Scott prepared it as a study skin.

There are two fall reports: Del Armstrong found one in a tree at the base of Mount Moroni on October 29, 1982, and J. Hertman found one in a water tank near Lava Point on October 2, 1990; it was rescued, dried, fed grasshoppers, and released.

Western Screech-Owl. *Otus kennicottii.*
Uncommon permanent resident.

Most reports are from the lowlands, especially Oak Creek Canyon and Springdale, but it occurs in the high country as well; Don and Carole Falvey reported one from Blue Springs Lake on December 9, 1993. There are three nesting records: Angus Woodbury first noted young birds in Zion Canyon in July 1930, Raymond Gifford reported an adult and an immature bird at Springdale on July 1, 1976, and Charles Torrance and Jerome Gifford found two adults and two immature birds there on July 4 and 6, 1977. Also, it was recorded on seven of 25 CBCs (1970–94), including a high count of three birds on December 27, 1994.

Two color phases have been recorded in the Zion Park Screech-Owls. Clifford Presnall (1935) was first to observe this; he found two birds, one reddish-brown and one gray, at the South Entrance on

January 27, 1935. The red color phase was not previously known for this species in the Southwest.

Great Horned Owl. *Bubo virginianus.*
Fairly common permanent resident.

This is the most commonly seen owl in the Zion Park area. Although most records are from the riparian woodlands, it has been reported at all elevations. Its deep hooting is most often heard during the spring and early summer. Nesting has been recorded on several occasions: I found a very young bird at Wylie Retreat on July 27, 1965; Jerome Gifford found a nest, containing at least three young, at Lava Point on June 4, 1978; he found another nest in a pothole in a cliff east of Rockville on May 4, 1979; and Dale Dockstader reported four juveniles at Rockville on July 14, 1979. Also it was recorded on 19 of 25 CBCs (1970–1994), including a high count of six birds on December 28, 1981.

Northern Pygmy-Owl. *Glaucidium gnoma.*
Uncommon year-round resident.

Although it has been reported most often at lowland sites, especially Springdale, from early October through January, it also has been recorded at a wide range of other localities. Nesting birds have been reported near the Zion Lodge on July 5, 1964 (an immature bird was found dead and preserved) (Wauer 1969); at the Grotto Picnic Area, where Peter Scott found an immature bird not able to fly on May 31, 1974; in Zion Canyon on July 23, 1976, where Lois Winter found a downy youngster; and in Hidden Canyon on July 14, 1979, where Steve Hedges reported a nesting pair with two young.

Jerome Gifford recorded arrival and departure dates at Springdale for five seasons: from December 2, 1976, to March 6, 1977; October 3, 1978, to January 23, 1979; December 20, 1982, to February 8, 1983; November 7, 1983, to January 26, 1984; November 12, 1984, to January 18, 1985. And one or two birds were reported on 16 of 25 CBCs (1970–1994). In addition, Robert Wood reported one with a captured White-crowned Sparrow at the ZCVC on December 20, 1975; and J. L. Crawford, Joel Fishbein, Victor Jackson, Peter Scott, and Robert Wood watched one trying to capture House Sparrows hiding under the eaves of the ZCVC on November 25, 1975.

Spotted Owl. *Strix occidentalis.*
Uncommon permanent resident.

This threatened species, often known as "Mexican Spotted Owl," frequents patches of dense forest that persist within the park's abundant narrow slot canyons and gorges, generally at mid-elevations. The Zion Park population is one of the largest on the Colorado Plateau.

There are numerous nesting records, beginning with an immature bird captured by Angus Woodbury in June 1928; Peter Scott watched an adult feeding a young bird along the Canyon Overlook Trail on July 22, 1974; Monica Speidel photographed two adults and an immature bird in Orderville Canyon on June 27, 1975; Ken Kertell reported a nest in 1976; and recent surveys by the NPS have produced many more nesting records. In 1995, Brent Hetzler (1995) and colleagues located 32 birds and documented 15 occupied territories—each ranging in size from 0.5 to 4.0 square miles—that produced a total of eight fledglings.

Nest sites usually are located in crevices in old debris sites on cliffs. Juveniles remain with the adults until September, when they normally leave the territory, sometimes moving a considerable distance. In winter, females usually remain on their territory, while males usually move to warmer (often higher) sites. It was recorded on only one of 25 CBCs (1970–94); David Ng photographed one at Watercress Spring on the Riverside Walk, December 27, 1977.

In a food preference study by David Willey (1995), an analysis of 47 pellets taken from nests revealed that woodrats made up 40% of the Spotted Owl's diet, White-footed Mice (19%); other small mammals such as cottontails, chipmunks, and bats (22%); insects (17%); and birds made up only about 1% of their diet. This nocturnal predator normally hunts from perches, moving to lower perches just before attacking its prey. And they sometimes cache their prey in trees or tall grass near logs or rock outcrops.

Long-eared Owl. *Asio otus.*
Two records.

Allan Hagood first discovered one in upper Coalpits Wash in mid-March 1965, and one was hit by a pick-up truck driven by Ray Williams near the East Entrance on April 1, 1978; this bird was retrieved and identified by Louise Excell, who gave the specimen to

Spotted Owl

the NPS. The two records probably do not give an accurate indication of its true status.

Northern Saw-whet Owl. *Aegolius acadicus.*
Sporadic resident.

These little owls apparently move into the Zion Park area and stay for a year or two before withdrawing; Jerome Gifford found that all of the Zion Park area records fell within four periods: 1933–36, 1963–65, 1974–76, and 1982–83. It has been reported for every month but November, although none were recorded on any of the 25 CBCs (1970–94). The first area record is two discovered "near the south boundary on October 15, 1933, by E. H. Cantrell, Jr., who collected one" that was later examined by Clifford Presnall (Presnall 1935). And in February 1936, one found in a pear tree in Springdale by Cantrell and Jerome Gifford was collected and mounted. All the later reports between Springdale and the Narrows have involved lone birds.

FAMILY CAPRIMULGIDAE:
GOATSUCKERS (NIGHTJARS)

Lesser Nighthawk. *Chordeiles acutipennis.*
Rare summer visitor.

It is a regular summer resident in the lower Virgin River Valley, and it occasionally wanders into the Zion Park area from late June to early September. In 1981, Jerome Gifford recorded it almost daily, and he recorded up to about 40 individuals at the Grafton Ponds from July 30 to August 10. The latest record is six near Rockville on September 2, 1964 (Dennis Carter). Specimens taken at Washington on May 7, 1965, and near Hurricane on June 2, 1966, represented the race *texensis* (Wauer 1969).

Common Nighthawk. *Chordeiles minor.*
Uncommon summer resident and fairly common migrant.

This is a late arrival; the earliest spring report is one at the mouth of Pine Creek Canyon on May 18, 1972 (Jerome Gifford). Reports increase from late May to mid-June, when it usually can be found in the lower valley and less often in Zion Canyon. Although there are no nesting records, it certainly must nest, at least in the high country. Shane Pruett and Matt Snyder reported three or four birds at Lava Point on July 1, 1993. By late July it can be common at all elevations as post-nesting birds and southbound migrants appear. At Grafton, Gifford recorded birds from July 25 to September 16, 1981, and from July 25 to October 5, 1983, with a high count of 167 birds "migrating high over Grafton to the southeast" (Gifford 1987) on August 11, 1981. There are scattered sightings to October 16.

Common Poorwill. *Phalaenoptilus nuttallii.*
Fairly common summer resident.

It has been recorded as early as April 2 and as late as October 26, primarily in the lowlands. But post-nesting birds may occur in the high country; one was even reported at 10,000 feet at Cedar Breaks on August 26, 1975. Most observations are of lone birds sitting along the roads at dusk and dawn; their eyes reflect a distinctly red glow. A drive along the Kolob Terrace Road from Virgin to Lava Point during a summer evening will usually produce several individuals.

Whip-poor-will. *Caprimulgus vociferus.*
Casual spring visitor.

It was first reported in Oak Creek Canyon on two consecutive nights in early May 1965 (Clyde and Lois Harden). Peter Scott next heard one singing with a Common Poorwill at Potato Hollow on May 8, 1976. It was reported at Springdale on April 4, 1980, by Merrill Webb; Joseph A. Hall heard one singing at Crystal Spring in Zion Canyon on the nights of May 13 and 14, 1981; and Roy Givens reported one near the ZCVC on April 8, 1986.

FAMILY APODIDAE: SWIFTS

Black Swift. *Cypseloides niger.*
Casual migrant.

There are three spring reports, one in July, and three fall reports. Spring sightings include one over Deertrap Mountain on May 11, 1964 (Wauer), another over Emerald Pools Canyon on May 31, 1992 (NPS files), and Tim Manns and Brenda Cunningham observed one over the Narrows on July 17, 1990. Fall records include a dead bird found below Weeping Rock by Guy Musser on August 2, 1960, another flying over Oak Creek Canyon on August 25, 1964 (Wauer), and Jerome Gifford observed nine individuals over Springdale on September 23, 1981. The Black Swift is considered "an uncommon summer resident in Utah where it is now known to breed in the Wasatch Mountains" (Hayward et al. 1976; Behle et al. 1985).

White-throated Swift. *Aeronautes saxatalis.*
Abundant summer resident and migrant; sporadic in winter.

This is one of Zion's most characteristic summer birds; it can almost always be found about the high cliffs, and its high-pitched calls are commonplace. Nesting occurs in high rock crevices; copulating pairs, clasped together and spinning downward as if out of control, can be seen often in spring and early summer. Spring arrivals normally appear in late March and birds remain at least until mid-October. Migrating flocks of up to 200 individuals can be expected. And a few individuals remain during mild winters, utilizing communal roosting sites in high crevices on south-facing cliffs and feeding over nearby fields and the lower, open canyons, such as Coalpits Wash, on warm, sunny days.

FAMILY TROCHILIDAE: HUMMINGBIRDS

Broad-billed Hummingbird. *Cynanthus latirostris.*
Two records.

Richard Fesler discovered an adult male at the Springdale feeder of Fred and Leo Fesler on October 1, 1978; Jerome Gifford saw the bird and photographed it on November 19, 21, and 23. Louise Excell observed it on November 21 and it was last seen by Richard Fesler on November 25. Then, on September 9 and 10, 1979, an adult male appeared at Gifford's feeder at Springdale. Gifford's photograph was later published in *Utah Birds* (Gifford 1986).

Magnificent Hummingbird. *Eugenes fulgens.*
Two records.

A lone female was found at feeders at Jerome Gifford's home in Springdale off and on from July 7 to August 9, 1971; he photographed it on July 11, 24, and 30, and a photograph was later published in *Utah Birds* (Gifford 1986). A second record, perhaps the same bird, fed regularly at Gifford's feeders from May 23 to August 8, 1972; it also was seen by Clyde and Lois Harden.

Black-chinned Hummingbird. *Archilochus alexandri.*
Abundant summer resident.

Records of this little lowland hummingbird extend from March 10 to October 14, and Jerome Gifford recorded it almost daily at Springdale during the following periods: March 18 to September 22, 1972; March 23 to October 6, 1974; and April 4 to October 14, 1975. He also recorded it from April 6 to September 30, 1975, with more than 100 individuals at his feeders constantly from April 25 to September 3; in 1980 he recorded them from April 2 to October 24, with 100 to 300 individuals at his feeders from May 14 to September 9; and he recorded it in 1982 from April 25 to September 20, with 100 to 300 at his feeders from April 17 to August 21. And in 1987, Gifford observed 450 to 550 Black-chins at his feeders during the last half of July, and 600 to 700 individuals on three stormy days.

There are numerous nesting records of this hummingbird, primarily in the riparian woodlands and all below approximately 4,500 feet elevation. Gifford found nests as early as May 4 and as late as July 31 in Springdale and on May 9 in Coalpits Wash. And there also is a single winter report: one at Springdale on the December 27, 1989, CBC.

Costa's Hummingbird. *Calypte costae.*
Uncommon spring resident.

The majority of records of this little desert hummingbird are from Coalpits and Huber Washes from late March to mid-May; the latest report is a lone male at Coalpits Wash on June 9, 1979 (Jerome Gifford). There also is a March 1, 1994, very early report at Springdale (C. McCollum). The Zion Park area is the northern edge of its range, and birds apparently leave the area soon after nesting.

Calliope Hummingbird. *Stellula calliope.*
Rare spring and fall migrant.

Spring records range from March 25 to May 30, with the majority of sightings reported from mid-April to early May. There are no June

Black-chinned Hummingbird

reports. Southbound birds may arrive as early as July 2 and linger to September 12, with the majority of the fall reports from mid-July to the end of August. And there is a very late sighting of a lone male coming to feeders at the John Voyles home in Springdale on November 6, 1973.

Broad-tailed Hummingbird. *Selasphorus platycercus.*
Fairly common summer resident and migrant.

It has been recorded as early as March 7 and as late as October 22, but the majority of sightings occur from early April to late July. This is the earliest hummingbird to appear in the spring, and breeding birds often proceed directly to high country sites. I discovered a nest on the underside of a moss-covered overhanging rock near Blue Springs Lake on June 9, 1965; the nest was built of moss and bits of lichen and spiderwebs, which offered excellent camouflage. And Jerome Gifford recorded territorial birds on three 40-acre breeding bird census plots: three pairs in the "slick-rock-ponderosa pine-pinyon-juniper" (Gifford 1981) habitat at the junction of Clear and Pine canyons from May 25 to July 20, 1980; three pairs in the pinyon-juniper woodland near the East Entrance from May 14 to July 15, 1977 and 1978; and two in the mixed pine-fir-aspen woodland near Lava Point from June 4 to July 24, 1978.

Migrants are most evident at lowland areas before and after nesting, and Gifford reported a significant influx of Broad-tails during an unseasonable snowstorm on May 6 and 7, 1965. Numbers increase in the lowlands by mid-July, and they are almost nonexistent in the highlands after mid-August. Lowland reports persist until mid-October.

Rufous Hummingbird. *Selasphorus rufus.*
Common late summer visitor.

Records of this aggressive little hummingbird range from mid-June to October 22; all these are post-nesting transients from breeding grounds further north. These summer transients can normally be found at flowering plants at all elevations. Jerome Gifford recorded birds at his Springdale feeders almost daily during six seasons: from July 5 to October 22, 1972, with a high of 90 on August 19 and 22; from July 16 to September 2, 1973; from June 28 to September 19, 1974; from June 19 to September 20, 1975. And in 1977, he recorded 200 individuals daily from August 22 to September 6; from July 13 to September 13, 1986; and from July 2 to October 4, 1987, with highs of 100 and 130 on August 26 and 27, respectively. Northbound birds migrate along the West Coast in spring.

FAMILY ALCEDINIDAE: KINGFISHERS

Belted Kingfisher. *Ceryle alcyon.*
Fairly common permanent resident.

This vociferous bird can be found along the Virgin River and at adjacent ponds year-round, although it tends to be rather secretive during the nesting season from late spring to mid-summer. Jerome

Belted Kingfisher

Gifford reported nesting burrows in banks at Grafton, north Springdale, the mouth of Zion Canyon, and in Birch Creek Canyon. It is most obvious from early September through mid-April, and CBC participants recorded it on all 25 CBCs (1970–94), with an average of four individuals and a high count of nine on December 28, 1981.

FAMILY PICIDAE: WOODPECKERS

Lewis' Woodpecker. *Melanerpes lewis.*
Sporadic fall and early winter visitor.

Records extend from September 23 to December 29, and there are two spring reports: Jerome Gifford found one at Springdale on April 30, 1973, and another at Grafton on April 16–19, 1985. Fall birds apparently visit the Zion Park area during years of good acorn crops; Andrea Brand reported 10 adults and juveniles on the West Rim, all collecting acorns from oaks and storing the acorns in a large ponderosa pine, on September 23, 1994; Jerome and Jewel Gifford and Merrill Webb found it present on the Kolob Terrace from September 28 to November 29, 1984, with a high of eight birds on October 12; and Dennis Carter and I found at least 20 birds at Potato Hollow on October 31, 1963. There also are three December reports: Jerome Gifford found lone birds at the East Entrance on December 26, 1975, and December 25, 1979; and Jeanne LeBer and Ray Smith found one near the West Rim cabin on December 29, 1987.

Acorn Woodpecker. *Melanerpes formicivorus.*
Casual visitor.

One found in Pine Valley on the Kolob Terrace on May 8, 1985, by Robert Bond, Steve Hedges, and James Tucker, represented the first verified record for Utah (Hedges 1985). However, there were two earlier reports: Phillip Sollins found one at Springdale on August 25, 1970, and Gene Trapp and seven other biology teachers and students found one at the West Rim Overlook on June 8, 1979. Eric Haskell reported two at Potato Hollow on May 26, 1994, and Terry Saddler observed one near Pine Valley in May 1995.

Red-naped Sapsucker. *Sphyrapicus nuchalis.*
Fairly common summer resident; common migrant; sporadic winter resident.

Several nesting records of this bird, earlier known as the Yellow-bellied Sapsucker, exist for the forested high country. A nest with young was found in an aspen at Potato Hollow on June 20, 1962 (Dennis Carter and Bruce Moorhead); I found a courting pair near Blue Springs Lake on June 1, 1965, and another pair nesting in an aspen on Carpenter Hill on June 9, 1965. Post-nesting birds usually remain in the high country until late September. Jerome Gifford recorded early and late arrivals at Springdale during five seasons: from September 24, 1979, to February 23, 1980; October 22, 1981, to February 7, 1982; October 5, 1982, to February 13, 1983; October 8, 1983, to February 5, 1984; and September 27, 1984, to February 11, 1985. And on September 24, 1995, I found six birds, which I assumed were migrating, moving south along Coalpits Wash.

Winter residents prefer orchards and riparian woodlands, but are somewhat sporadic in occurrence. I banded 31 individuals in Zion Canyon during the winter of 1962–63, but only eight and 15 in 1963–64 and 1964–65, respectively. And although CBC participants recorded an average of eight birds on 25 counts (1970–94), only one was recorded in 1970, 1971, and 1972, while a high of 38 was tallied on December 27, 1988.

Williamson's Sapsucker. *Sphyrapicus thyroideus.*
Casual fall migrant and winter visitor.

The majority of reports range from mid-September through December, but there also are two spring and/or early summer records: Jerome Gifford found one at Springdale on April 27, 1975, and Greer Chesher reported a male at Lava Point on June 23, 1983. The earliest fall sighting is a female at Emerald Pools on September 16, 1982 (Melanie Madsen); I found one at Potato Hollow on September 27, 1965; Gifford observed a female at Springdale on October 22, 1982, and a female utilizing "feeding holes in a Siberian elm . . . that had been excavated by a male Yellow-bellied [Red-naped] Sapsucker" (Gifford 1987) there from November 4 to 13, 1982; and Russ Grater reported one on the West Rim on November 15, 1941. There are two

December reports: Clyde and Lois Harden found a dead bird at Zion Lodge on December 8, 1964, and J. L. Crawford recorded a male in Springdale on the December 27, 1985, CBC.

Ladder-backed Woodpecker. *Picoides scalaris.*
Rare winter visitor.

Several records exist for the Zion Park lowlands, especially from the desert environment in Coalpits Wash and the Grafton/Rockville area, from early November to mid-March. And it has been recorded on 17 of 25 CBCs (1970–94), including high counts of five individuals on December 27, 1985, and December 27, 1990. There are four additional reports: Jerome Gifford found lone birds in Coalpits Wash on May 1, 1981, and at Springdale on May 18, 1984; Lynn Ballard reported a lone male at Grafton on August 21, 1978; and Dennis Carter found a female or immature bird in Coalpits Wash on September 18, 1964.

Downy Woodpecker. *Picoides pubescens.*
Fairly common permanent resident.

This tiny-billed woodpecker resides in the riparian woodlands in the lowlands as well as in aspen communities in the high country; there appears to be some movement into warmer areas during severe winters. And there are several nesting records: Richard Foerster found it nesting in Springdale on April 16, 1974; Jerome Gifford photographed a pair at a nesting tree in Springdale on June 11, 1978; and he recorded one pair in a 25-acre breeding bird census plot in the Watchman Campground in both 1981 and 1982. Highland nesting records include one in an aspen at Indian Hollow, near Kolob Reservoir, on June 7, 1952 (Gifford); Dennis Carter and I found a nest with young in an aspen grove in Potato Hollow on June 27, 1963; and I found another nest in an aspen on Carpenter Hill on May 27, 1965.

During the winter months, it may be somewhat sporadic in the lowlands, depending upon weather conditions. Although it was never missed on 25 CBCs (1970–94), count numbers ranged from one, two, or three individuals on six years to ten or more bird on eight years; a high count of 23 birds was recorded on December 27, 1994.

Hairy Woodpecker. *Picoides villosus.*
Common permanent resident.

This is the most common woodpecker of the Zion Park area, and it occurs in all forest/woodland habitats about equally. Nests have been reported for all elevations: Jerome Gifford found two breeding pairs on 40-acre breeding bird census plots at the East Entrance in 1977, 1978, and 1979; I found a nesting pair in Potato Hollow on June 27, 1963; Jerome Gifford found a nesting pair at the Grotto Picnic Area on July 15, 1972; and Cindy Beaudett found a pair nesting in a cottonwood at the Watchman Campground on May 2, 1983.

There appears to be only minor movement into lowland areas in winter, and only during stormy periods. Christmas Bird Count participants recorded an average of eight individuals over 25 years (1970–94), one to three birds on five counts, and ten or more on eight years; a high count of 20 birds was recorded on December 27, 1982.

Northern Flicker. *Colaptes auratus.*
Fairly common summer resident and migrant; abundant winter resident.

This large, ground-feeding woodpecker nests in woodland/forest habitats at all elevations: Jerome Gifford recorded nesting birds at Grafton, Rockville, Springdale, Zion Canyon, the Narrows, Hidden Canyon, and Lava Point from 1978 through 1982. J. L. and Fern Crawford reported a pair nesting in a dead cottonwood stump in the Grotto Picnic Area on April 1, 1993, and I found adults feeding young on Deertrap Mountain on June 22, 1965.

Lowland birds usually move to higher elevations by May, returning by early October with the southbound migrants that increase in numbers through November. Winter populations are reasonably stable; CBC participants recorded it every year (1970–94), averaging 50 birds, with low numbers of 12, 19, and 20, and high counts of 121 and 74.

Resident flickers demonstrate a surprisingly high degree of intergradation between the red-shafted and yellow-shafted races (these were separate species until they were lumped together by the AOU in 1983). In fact, Gifford's examination of 27 flickers found in Zion Canyon in the spring of 1982 revealed that 55% showed some indication of intergradation; five had yellow wing-linings (Gifford 1987).

In addition, I had a fascinating experience with a pair of flickers in Oak Creek Canyon on November 14, 1964. A female, that had been caught in the lower strand of my mist net, was loudly protesting, while a male, standing immediately below it on the ground, was also calling and tugging at the female with clasped bills. After seven or eight tugs, the male jumped onto the body of the female and began pecking at the net strands, all the time calling in a loud manner typical of an annoyed flicker. He then jumped back onto the ground and again clasped the female's bill with his and began backing away, with the help of wing beats, apparently trying to pull the female free of the net. He suddenly released his hold and flew at the net. He again jumped on her body and began a vigorous pecking at the net strands. Just as suddenly, he jumped back onto the ground and began the tugging process again. I then retracted, banded, and released the female, which flew to a nearby rock where it began loud, constant calling. It was immediately answered by the male. Within 30 seconds he flew to her and they disappeared up-canyon together (Wauer 1965b).

FAMILY TYRANNIDAE: TYRANT FLYCATCHERS

Olive-sided Flycatcher. *Contopus borealis.*
Uncommon summer resident and fairly common migrant.

It has been recorded as early as April 29 (one in Steven's Canyon by Jerome Gifford) to September 17; the majority of reports, however, range from mid-May to late July. Migrants can be expected almost anywhere and at all elevations, but breeding birds utilize only high country sites. On June 15, 1965, I found six singing, presumably breeding adults, at Carpenter Hill, Blue Springs Lake, Lava Point, Potato Hollow, at the Great West Canyon Overlook, and at the West Rim cabin. And Gifford recorded one territorial pair on a 40-acre breeding bird census plot at Lava Point from June 4 to July 24, 1978.

Post-nesting birds usually leave their breeding territories by the end of July, but post-nesting birds and migrants linger at various choice sites. Steve and Priscilla Summers found five individuals along the Kolob Terrace Road on August 14, 1995, and Gifford

Western Wood-Pewee

reported birds at Grafton and Springdale from August 20 to September 17.

Western Wood-Pewee. *Contopus sordidulus.*
Abundant summer resident and fairly common migrant.

This is one of Zion's most characteristic birds. In summer it is numerous in the riparian woodlands in the lowlands, but it also resides in forested habitats in the high country. There are several nesting records: Jerome Gifford recorded breeding birds at Grafton, Springdale, Watchman Campground, upper Pine Canyon, Hidden Canyon, and Lava Point in 1974, 1976, 1978, and 1981; Dennis Carter found a nest, with an incubating adult, on a Douglas fir near Lava Point on June 20, 1963; and Richard A. Stuart reported a nest, with three young, at the Kolob Reservoir on August 18, 1971. Post-nesting birds and migrants usually remain in the high country through August, but they have been reported only from the lowlands during September, and Gifford found two late migrants at Springdale on October 2, 1974.

Willow Flycatcher. *Empidonax traillii.*
Rare summer resident.

The race of this little flycatcher, often called "Southwestern" Willow Flycatcher, is listed as endangered by the federal government. It appears that the local breeding population has declined in recent years, although it may never have been common. Clifford Presnall (1935) noted it first "in willow thickets in Zion Canyon and Shunes Creek Canyon" in May, June, and July. By the 1960s, Dennis Carter and I (Wauer and Carter 1965) reported one "along the Virgin River at the mouth of Parunuweap Canyon, June 23, 1964 (Carter), one collected at the Springdale Ponds, May 10, 1965 (Wauer), and one seen at the Springdale Ponds, June 27, 1965 (Russell)"; and there are two additional 1965 records: I banded one in Oak Creek Canyon on May 5 (early season date) and another at Springdale on May 25.

During the last 30 years, it was reported only four times: Jerome Gifford found a nest at the Springdale Ponds on May 30, 1976, another was "seen regularly during June [1979] in south Springdale" (Gifford 1987), and he reported one at Springdale on September 18, 1983; and a territorial male was observed in "dense willow thicket, framed by cottonwoods" (NPS files) in Parunuweap Canyon by Steve Hedges and Sheri Fedorchak on June 6, 1994.

Hammond's Flycatcher. *Empidonax hammondii.*
Rare migrant.

This little *Empidonax* is extremely difficult to identify in the field, except when it is singing on its nesting grounds; otherwise, positive identification requires measurements. From 1963 to 1966, I banded birds at the Springdale Ponds on September 2, 1964, and May 17, 1965, and I banded one in Oak Creek Canyon on September 2, 1965; I collected one in Oak Creek Canyon on May 15, 1963, and another at Springdale on May 6, 1965. It probably is more numerous in migration than these few records suggest.

Dusky Flycatcher. *Empidonax oberholseri.*
Fairly common summer resident and migrant.

This is the *Empidonax* that resides in conifer and aspen habitats in the high country and in the cool side-canyons below the high terraces. Nests have been reported on an aspen on Carpenter Hill on June 1, 1965, and on a cottonwood in Oak Creek Canyon on June 15, 1965 (Wauer). Jerome Gifford found a nest in Refrigerator Canyon on July 25, 1976. During May and again in August and September, it is the most common flycatcher in the lower canyons and along the Virgin River Valley. From August 1963 to late July 1966, I banded 22 individuals between April 30 (earliest record) and May 26 at Springdale and Oak Creek Canyon, and two in September, both at the Watchman Campground on September 15 and 26 (latest record).

Gray Flycatcher. *Empidonax wrightii.*
Uncommon summer resident.

Records of this little flycatcher, which nests in the pinyon-juniper woodland, extend from April 27 (one found in Oak Creek Canyon by Wauer) to two individuals found on the Watchman Trail on August 31, 1980 (Jerome Gifford). Nesting was documented on a breeding bird census plot at the East Entrance by Gifford: territorial pairs were present from May 14 to July 15, 1978, and from May 22 to July 22, 1979. An August 26, 1971, report by Richard A. Stuart at the Kolob Reservoir may represent either migration or post-nesting dispersal.

This little *Empidonax* flycatcher can readily be identified in the field, even away from its breeding grounds, by its tail-dipping behavior: this "movement begins with a rapid, very slight upward twitch of the tail, followed by a slower, emphasized downward swing, after which the tail is raised to its original position" (Kaufman 1990).

Cordilleran Flycatcher. *Empidonax occidentalis.*
Fairly common summer resident and migrant.

This yellowish *Empidonax* does not arrive in the Zion Park area until the first of May and it leaves its nesting grounds by mid-July. Jerome Gifford recorded one nesting pair on a 50-acre breeding bird census plot in Heaps' Canyon on two consecutive years: from May 1 to July 17, 1982, and May 27 to July 16, 1983. Also, a nest with eggs was found on a ledge in a rock crevice along the Riverside Walk on June 25, 1962 (Dennis Carter); pairs of territorial birds were found in Refrigerator Canyon and near Blue Springs Lake all during June 1965 (Wauer); and Ken Kertell found two nests in 1974: one "about 30 ft. up a vertical rock face and was placed on top of what appeared to be a clump of club moss" in Refrigerator Canyon on June 27, and another "located about 3 ft. up under a sandstone ledge. It was composed of grasses and dead leaves. It contained at least 2 young and probably 3" (NPS files).

Spring migrants can be common in the lowlands; I banded 14 individuals in Oak Creek Canyon from May 7 to 14, 1965. And in 1965, Clyde and Lois Harden banded six at the Lamoreoux Ranch along the Kolob Reservoir Road from July 17 to 27. There is one later report: Gifford reported one on the Kolob Terrace on August 6, 1983.

This western species, previously known as Western Flycatcher, was split into two species by the AOU in 1989: the Pacific-slope Flycatcher of the West Coast and the Cordilleran Flycatcher of the Interior. This bird can also be identified in the field by its obviously yellowish throat, olive-green back, and distinct eye-ring that is elongated toward the back.

Black Phoebe. *Sayornis nigricans.*
Uncommon permanent resident.

In summer, this all-black flycatcher, except for a white belly, can be found along the Virgin River and adjacent ponds up to the Narrows. But the Zion Canyon birds withdraw into the lower, warmer valley in winter. I found a nest under construction at the Springdale Ponds on March 15, 1965; it was later deserted and another nest was built nearby where nesting activity was evident through May, and young were seen on May 25. Peter Scott found a nest at the Watchman Campground on May 25, 1974; Jerome Gifford found nesting birds there from July 1 to 11, 1982, and again from June 5 to 27, 1986; he also found them at Springdale from April 23 to July 10, 1978, and at Grafton from May 13 to July 15, 1979.

Winter birds can almost always be found along the Virgin River below the mouth of Zion Canyon. It has been missed on only five of 25 CBCs (1970–94), with high counts of four individuals recorded on December 27, 1984, and December 27, 1985.

Black Phoebe

Eastern Phoebe. *Sayornis phoebe.*
Four records.

The earliest and first report for Utah was one found in the Watchman Campground by Dennis Carter and Allegra Collister on October 21 and 22, 1963. A second record was one collected at the Springdale Ponds on March 27, 1965, and a third bird was collected there on December 17, 1965 (Wauer 1966b). There is one other very unusual and late report: Jerome Gifford found three individuals near the East Entrance on May 13, 1964.

Say's Phoebe. *Sayornis saya.*
Common summer resident and migrant; uncommon in winter.

Summer residents can be found at all elevations. I found a nest with a single egg in Coalpits Wash on April 6, 1963; another nest, containing four fledglings, at Springdale on May 16, 1965; and one with young at the bridge near the ZCVC on May 25, 1965. Jerome Gifford recorded territorial pairs on three breeding bird census plots in 1979: three pairs in a 60-acre plot at Grafton from May 13 to July 15; 2.5 pairs on a 160-acre plot in Coalpits Wash from April 15 to July 2; and one pair on a 40-acre plot at the East Entrance from May 22 to July 22. Gifford also found nests on the Zion Inn (now Nature Center) from April 12 to 17, 1972, at Springdale from June 17 to July 6, 1973, and two in Coalpits Wash: one from March 31 to April 28, 1974, and another from April 28 to July 14, 1974. And Alice Galleys reported a nest on the bridge near the ZCVC on June 23, 1974.

Spring migrants can be expected in early March, and numbers increase during the remainder of the month; a high of 15-plus individuals was recorded at Springdale on March 25, 1965 (Wauer). Post-nesting and fall migrants may occur at all elevations from mid-August to mid-October. And winter birds are most numerous in the fields and desert slopes in the lowlands. Winter birds may be somewhat sporadic in occurrence; the Say's Phoebe was recorded on 21 of 25 CBCs (1970–94), with an average of five individuals and high counts of 11, 10, and 9 birds on December 17, 1973, December 27, 1983, and December 28, 1993, respectively.

Ash-throated Flycatcher. *Myiarchus cinerascens.*
Common summer resident and uncommon migrant.

Records of this mid-sized flycatcher extend from April 23 to August 31; Jerome Gifford recorded it almost daily at Springdale from April 29 to August 3, 1980, and April 26 to July 16, 1981. During this period it is the area's most common flycatcher. Nest-building was observed in Oak Creek Canyon the first week of May in 1964 and 1965 (Wauer); young were being fed by adults there on June 17, 1965 (Al Walent); and Gifford recorded territorial pairs on each of five breeding bird census plots: two pairs on a 160-acre plot in Coalpits Wash from April 15 to July 2, 1979; two pairs on a 60-acre plot at Grafton from May 13 to July 15, 1979; two pairs on a 26-acre plot at the Springdale Ponds from April 23 to July 10, 1978; one pair on a 40-acre plot at the confluence of Pine and Clear Creeks from May 25 to July 20, 1980; three pairs on a 40-acre plot at the East Entrance from May 14 to July 18, 1978, and again from May 22 to July 22, 1979. In addition, in 1978 in the South Campground, Gifford found Ash-throated Flycatchers nesting in three cavities that had been utilized by Western Bluebirds the previous year.

Western Kingbird

Cassin's Kingbird. *Tyrannus vociferans.*
Uncommon summer resident and migrant.

It has been recorded as early as February 20 (Jerome Gifford found one at Springdale in 1973), there are a few sightings during March and April, but it cannot be expected with certainty until the first week of May. Nesting records include a territorial pair near Firepit Knoll all during June 1965 (Wauer), and Gifford recorded two territorial pairs on a 40-acre breeding bird census plot at the East Entrance from June 5 to July 31, 1977, May 14 to July 15, 1978, and May 22 to July 22, 1979. The East Entrance birds may remain through July, then either move out of the area entirely or join southbound birds in the lowlands; Gifford has recorded Cassin's Kingbirds at Springdale and Grafton all during August and as late as September 16.

Western Kingbird. *Tyrannus verticalis.*
Common summer resident.

This is the kingbird commonly found in the lowland riparian habitat along the Virgin River and also in residential areas from Rockville to

Springdale and the Watchman, where they often nest on brackets and transformers on utility poles. There are numerous nesting records: Jerome Gifford found nesting birds at Springdale from May 23 to July 11, 1965, and May 14 to July 10, 1978; at Grafton from May 13 to July 15, 1979; and at the South Campground from May 22 to June 18, 1982.

Early arrivals may appear in mid-March, but they cannot be expected until the second week of April; Gifford reported a high count of 25 individuals at Springdale on April 10. He recorded birds at Springdale almost daily from April 15 to September 21, 1974, and from April 21 to September 9, 1975. There is little evidence of migration, although early and late birds may be migrants.

Family Alaudidae: Larks

Horned Lark. *Eremophila alpestris.*
Uncommon winter resident and casual migrant.

It cannot be expected anywhere within the park, but it usually can be found on the open desert flats—such as the Big Plains five miles south of Rockville—throughout the winter months from mid-December to mid-February. And during severe winter storms, many move into the more protected canyons. During 25 years of CBCs (1970–94), it was recorded only six times, including a high count of 400 individuals on December 27, 1988. Other high numbers of wintering birds include 70 in Coalpits Wash on December 26, 1974, and 150 at Springdale on February 7, 1979 (Jerome Gifford). And there are several reports of obvious migrants: Gifford found approximately 800 on the Big Plains on September 19, 1981; I recorded 30 to 40 individuals in Cave Valley on October 31, 1963, a flock of 16 birds at the East Entrance on November 7, 1963, a flock of about 12 birds in Cave Valley on February 22, 1965, and 220 at the East Entrance on February 25, 1965. Jerome Gifford recorded it twice in May: at Springdale on May 1, 1983, and at Cave Valley on May 21, 1985. He also reported that during the winter months it is the single "most abundant bird along the Antelope Spring-Hamilton Fort route" (Gifford 1987) just west of the Kolob Canyons.

Family Hirundinidae: Swallows

Tree Swallow. *Tachcineta bicolor.*
Common summer resident and spring migrant; rare fall migrant.
Records extend from early March to October 20, and there also is a single December report: Jerome Gifford found one at the Grafton Ponds on December 12, 1984. He recorded arrival and departure dates at Grafton on three seasons: from March 8 to May 18, 1983, with a high of 100 on April 4; March 17 to May 11, 1984, with a high of 200 on April 26 (good examples of spring migration); and March 14, through the summer months, to September 26, 1986. Although this species was present in 1986 all summer, there was no evidence of nesting.

Nesting occurs only in the high country in the vicinity of Blue Springs Lake and the Kolob Reservoir. I found a nest in an aspen at Blue Springs Lake on June 1, 1965, and I banded five of several dozen birds there on August 30 and 31, 1965. Post-nesting birds leave their breeding grounds by early September, and fall migrants can occasionally be found again at lowland sites. On the evening of September 22, 1995, I observed 26 individuals fly-catching over Oak Creek Canyon; they soon moved out over the Virgin River and disappeared down-river. Fall migrants usually remain on the upper terraces, dropping into the lowlands only during stormy weather.

Violet-green Swallow. *Tachycineta thalassina.*
Abundant summer resident and migrant.
This is the swallow commonly seen all summer in Zion Canyon and in the high country; records extend from early March until mid-October: Louise Excell reported one at Springdale on March 4, 1984, and Jerome Gifford found 40 individuals at the Grafton Ponds on October 16 and 18, 1981. Nesting occurs at all elevations and in a variety of locations: cavities in snags and living trees, especially in cottonwoods along the Virgin River, ponderosa pines at mid-elevations, and aspens at higher elevations; crevices in cliffs; and Gifford found Violet-greens nesting in abandoned Cliff Swallow nests at Grafton.

Migrants are most numerous from late March through May in the spring, and from mid-August through September in the fall. High counts include 500 at Grafton on April 29, 1983, and again

Violet-green Swallow

on May 27, 1981 (Gifford); 200 at Springdale on September 9, 1976 (Ken Kertell); and 350 at Springdale on September 13, 1982 (Gifford).

Northern Rough-winged Swallow. *Stelgidopteryx serripennis.*
Fairly common summer resident; abundant spring and rare fall migrant.

Records extend from March 20, through the summer months, to October 16, all from the lowlands, except for one banded at the Lamoreoux Ranch on July 17, 1965 (Clyde and Lois Harden). Nesting birds occur at dirt banks in Coalpits Wash and all along the Virgin River to the mouth of Zion Canyon. Jerome Gifford recorded it on three breeding bird census plots: four territorial pairs on a 26-acre plot at Springdale from April 23 to July 10, 1978; three territorial pairs on a 160-acre plot in Coalpits Wash from April 15 to July 2, 1979; and one territorial pair on a 60-acre plot at Grafton from May 13 to July 15, 1979.

Spring migrants are most numerous from early April to mid-May; Clyde and Lois Harden and I banded 46 Rough-wings at the Springdale Ponds from April 2 to May 15, 1965, compared with 42

Violet-green Swallows during this same period. High spring counts include 300 at Grafton on May 1, 1983, and 250 there on May 16, 1983 (Gifford). Fall migrants are most numerous from mid-August to mid-September, and there is a second spurt of migrants in mid-October; high counts of 40 birds were recorded on August 10, 1981, and October 15, 1980 (Gifford).

Bank Swallow. *Riparia riparia.*
Rare spring migrant.

Records range from April 11 to May 9, all in the lowlands at the Grafton Ponds and in nearby Coalpits Wash; the highest count was seven at Grafton on April 19, 1982 (Jerome Gifford). And Gifford observed one entering a hole in a gravel bank in Coalpits Wash on April 11, 1976; there is no further evidence of nesting, although nesting is possible and may occur. There also is a single fall report: Gifford found two birds at Grafton on September 24, 1986.

Cliff Swallow. *Hirundo pyrrhonota.*
Common summer resident and uncommon migrant.

Records extend from March 28, through the summer months, to October 20; Jerome Gifford observed it almost daily at Springdale from March 28 to October 14, 1981. Nesting colonies occur at localized places, such as on cliffs and under bridges, in Parunuweap Canyon, along the Virgin River in the vicinity of Grafton, Rockville, and Springdale, and at the mouth of Zion Canyon, where Gifford found 29 nests on July 11, 1980. His high count was 67 individuals at Grafton on June 28, 1981. Migrants may appear anywhere, although they are most numerous at water areas in the lowlands. Additional locations where migrants have been reported include Cave Valley, Blue Springs Lake, and Lava Point.

Barn Swallow. *Hirundo rustica.*
Uncommon migrant.

Spring records extend from March 18 (Jerome Gifford found two at the Grafton Ponds in 1987) to May 8, and fall records range from September 9 to October 16. All of these reports are from the lowlands at Grafton and adjacent Coalpits Wash. High counts include

58 and 42 on October 1 and October 3, 1981, respectively. During the last week of September 1986, a large migrating flock took refuge from strong, cold winds at Grafton; a high of 327 birds was recorded on September 27 (Gifford). In addition, Vasco Tanner (1927) reported that this species nested in old buildings in Zion Canyon, but there have been no similar reports since then.

Family Corvidae: Jays, Magpies, and Crows

Steller's Jay. *Cyanocitta stelleri.*
Common permanent resident.

This is the jay of the high country, although it also is found at localized areas below the high terraces, such as along the Narrows and at Emerald Pools. It also moves into the warmer lowlands during periods of severe winter weather and invasion years such as 1972–73, when they stayed into April; Gifford found birds "even as far out into the desert as Virgin" (Kingery 1973), and a high count of 20-plus individuals at Springdale on January 28. In 1979, storms on March 5 and 6 forced birds into the canyons; Gifford found 30 at Springdale. Nesting occurs only in pine-fir habitats; Gifford recorded three territorial pairs on a 40-acre breeding bird census plot at Lava Point from June 4 to July 24, 1978.

Western Scrub-Jay. *Aphelocoma californica.*
Common permanent resident.

Except in the dense forested areas in the high country, where the Steller's Jay is dominant, this is the most numerous jay at all elevations. I found adults feeding young among the Gambel's oaks along the West Rim Trail on May 19, 1965; an adult was seen feeding a single juvenile along Taylor Creek on May 21, 1964; and birds were feeding young at the Watchman residential area on May 19, 1965. Jerome Gifford recorded territorial pairs on two 40-acre breeding bird census plots: 0.5-pair in the "slickrock ponderosa pine-pinyon-juniper woodland" (Gifford 1981) at the confluence of Pine and Clear Creeks from May 25 to July 20, 1980; and he recorded one pair in the pinyon-juniper woodland at the East Entrance from May 22 to July 22, 1979.

In winter, it is most numerous in the lowlands; some high-country birds apparently move into the warmer canyons, especially during stormy weather. An average of 23 individuals were recorded on 25 CBCs (1970–94), including low counts of two and three birds in 1993 and 1970, respectively, and a high count of 73 on December 27, 1990.

The earlier name—Scrub Jay—was changed to Western Scrub-Jay by the AOU in 1996, when the one species was divided into three: Western Scrub-Jay of the West, Santa Cruz Island Scrub-Jay, and Florida Scrub-Jay.

Pinyon Jay. *Gymnorhinus cyanocephalus.*
Sporadic visitor.

This vociferous jay has been recorded year-round and at all elevations, yet there is no evidence of nesting. It is most often reported during the fall and winter months, when flocks of a few individuals to a hundred or more roam the mid-elevation slopes in search of ripe pinyon pine nuts. High counts of 100 to 150 birds were reported over Dennett Canyon on September 24, 1994 (Sheri Fedorchak); 100 were found at Springdale on November 10, 1972 (Ladessa Miller and Eunice Yager); and Jerome Gifford reported 100 birds at Springdale on March 1 to 12, 1980, and 150 there on April 3, 1980. In winter, it has been recorded on 20 of 25 CBCs (1970–94), with an average of 52 individuals and high counts of 100 or more in December 1972, 1973, and 1989.

Clark's Nutcracker. *Nucifraga columbiana.*
Sporadic fall, winter, and spring visitor.

Records extend from August 29 (one found at Camp Creek by Harry Schneider in 1991) to March 31 (I found one near Weeping Rock in 1966). Its occurrence in the Zion Park area is unpredictable, although it occasionally remains in one area for a considerable period; Jerome Gifford recorded it on a winter bird census plot in Heaps' Canyon several times from December 17, 1982, to February 15, 1983. And one or two birds were recorded on four of 25 CBCs (1970–94), in December 1972, 1988, 1991, and 1992. Numbers rarely exceed more than two or three birds, but Eric Haskell reported "several" at the West Rim from September 30 to October 3, 1994

Clark's Nutcracker

(NPS files), and I found five individuals at Lava Point on October 2, 1995. This boreal species nests at Cedar Breaks, and its presence in the Zion Park area at any time other than during the nesting season should be expected.

Black-billed Magpie. *Pica pica.*
Casual visitor.

There are six reports from the eastern edge of the park, principally along the North Fork Road, and Jerome Gifford reported one 14 miles beyond the East Entrance on January 19, 1975; it is resident in the Sevier Valley to the east. In addition, Clifford Presnall reported "several near Zion Lodge in May, 1935" (Presnall 1935), and three were found near Grafton during the December 28, 1978, CBC.

American Crow. *Corvus brachyrhynchos.*
Rare permanent resident.

Until the 1970s, this was a casual visitor to the Zion Park area, with records only in the lower Virgin River Valley, and 12 individuals were found near the mouth of Taylor Creek on January 14, 1965 (Wauer). In the 1980s, a pair regularly visited a feeder at the home of Doyle Winder in Oak Creek Canyon, and since about 1982 three to four young have been fledged annually. In 1987, Jerome Gifford recorded it almost daily in Springdale from June 11 to July 15, and he reported high counts of nine birds at Grafton on February 29, and seven at Springdale on June 22 and 23, 1984. More recently, I found a flock of 10 birds in the Rockville fields on October 11, 1995. And there also is one high country report: Robert Bond, Steve Hedges, and James Tucker observed a lone Crow near the Kolob Reservoir on May 8, 1985.

Common Raven. *Corvus corax.*
Common permanent resident.

This large, heavy-billed corvid occurs at all elevations year-round. A nest and adults were found in a rock crevice in Cave Valley on April 29, 1963 (Wauer); adults were seen feeding young near the ZCVC on June 28, 1965 (Al Walent); adults and four fledglings were perched on a ponderosa pine snag along the North Fork Road on July 6, 1965 (Bruce Moorhead and Wauer); Jerome Gifford found a nest in Wylie Retreat on June 22, 1972; and Andy Young reported a nest on a cliff near the East Entrance on May 25, 1994.

The majority of sightings are of one or two individuals or family groups, but I observed a flock of 60 individuals over Taylor Creek on May 13, 1964, and Gifford found 33 birds on the Big Plains, south of Rockville, on September 19, 1981. And it was reported on all 25 CBCs (1970–94), with an average of 22 individuals, low counts of four in December 1970, 1971, 1973, and 1977, and high counts of 54 and 53 birds on December 27, 1982, and December 27, 1993, respectively.

There also is a fascinating report of a Raven that flew into an open automobile window on the switchbacks below the Mt. Carmel Tunnel on July 4, 1995; driver Vincent Lu reported that he "opened door and it flew out" (NPS files). Sometimes this all-black bird is misidentified as a Golden Eagle or Peregrine Falcon from a distance; however, its wedge-shaped tail and heavy bill help separate this large bird from other less numerous soaring birds.

FAMILY PARIDAE: TITMICE

Black-capped Chickadee. *Parus atricapillus.*
Common permanent resident.

This handsome bird resides in riparian areas along the Virgin River and side-canyons and in aspen and oak groves in the high country. A pair of Black-caps nested in a hollowed log being used as a suet feeder in Oak Creek Canyon on June 5, 1965 (Clyde and Lois Harden); an adult was seen feeding young at Potato Hollow on June 27, 1963 (Wauer). Jerome Gifford reported nesting at the Watchman Campground from July 5 to 11, 1981, and again from May 26 to July 1, 1982; in Heaps' Canyon from May 7 to 13, 1983; and along the Narrows Trail from June 10 to July 14, 1983.

There appears to be some increase in lowland populations in winter, at least during stormy weather. An average of 37 individuals were recorded on 25 CBCs (1970–94), including low counts of ten or less only three times and high counts of 75 birds or more in December 1978 (78), 1991 (88), and 1992 (120).

Mountain Chickadee. *Parus gambeli.*
Common permanent resident.

This is the chickadee of the forested high country, although it often wanders into the lowlands in winter. I found a nest, with adults feeding young, on the West Rim on May 19, 1965; another nest, with an incubating adult, was found in an aspen on Carpenter Hill on June 9, 1965 (Wauer and Hardens); and Jerome Gifford recorded three territorial pairs on a 40-acre breeding bird census plot at Lava Point from June 4 to July 24, 1978.

Although it is most common in the high country and at niches of fir and pine in side-canyons, 14 individuals were banded in Oak Creek Canyon and the Watchman Campground from October 4 to March 7, 1963 (Wauer and Hardens). And it was recorded on 21 of 25 CBCs (1970–94), with a high count of 107 birds on December 28, 1981.

Plain Titmouse. *Parus inornatus.*
Common permanent resident.

This little crested tit resides almost exclusively in the pinyon-juniper woodlands, although it may also utilize adjacent broadleaf vegetation.

An adult was seen carrying food to young in a nest in a Gambel's oak on the slope of Firepit Knoll on June 9, 1965 (Wauer and Hardens). I found a pair feeding young on Deertrap Mountain on June 22, 1965. Jerome Gifford recorded territorial birds on two 40-acre breeding bird census plots: four pairs at the confluence of Pine and Clear Creeks from May 25 to July 29, 1980, and three pairs at the East Entrance from May 22 to July 22, 1979. There is little movement to lowland sites in winter, although it was missed on only three of 25 CBCs (1970–94); a high count of 24 was recorded on December 17, 1973.

Although the Plain Titmouse resides in the pinyon-juniper woodlands year-round, it can be difficult to find. Its very distinct calls—a scolding "see-jert-jert"—may help to locate it.

FAMILY AEGITHALIDAE: LONG-TAILED TITS AND BUSHTITS

Bushtit. *Psaltriparus minimus.*
Common permanent resident.

This tiny bird occurs at all elevations, although it is most numerous in the pinyon-juniper woodlands in summer and the riparian habitats along the Virgin River in winter. I discovered nests along the Weeping Rock Trail on May 2, 1963, and another under construction near Sleepy Hollow on May 19, 1965; adults were seen feeding nestlings below Maloney Hill on June 9, 1965 (Wauer and Hardens). Jerome Gifford recorded territorial pairs on two 40-acre breeding bird census plots: five pairs were recorded in the "slickrock ponderosa pine-pinyon-juniper woodland" (Gifford 1981) at the confluence of Pine and Clear Creeks from May 25 to July 20, 1980; and three pairs were recorded at the East Entrance from May 22 to July 22, 1979.

Post-nesting birds remain in family groups for several months, often joining other family groups and forming large flocks; Sheri Fedorchak found a flock of approximately 30 individuals in Parunuweap Canyon on October 20, 1992. And on 25 CBCs (1970–94), it was missed only in December 1979; 200 or more birds were recorded five times: December 1982 (274), 1988 (205), 1991

(445), 1992 (471), and 1994 (228). A few juveniles usually remain with the adults during their first full year, serving as "helpers" with nest-construction and feeding nestlings.

FAMILY SITTIDAE: NUTHATCHES

Red-breasted Nuthatch. *Sitta canadensis.*
Uncommon summer resident; sporadic visitor during fall, winter, and spring.
It can be expected with regularity only in summer in the high country, where it nests in pine-fir stands and aspen groves: an adult was observed feeding young and another adult was found incubating in a nest in an aspen on Carpenter Hill on June 1, 1965 (Wauer); another nest in an aspen was found near Blue Springs Lake on June 9, 1965 (Wauer and Hardens).

There is some post-nesting dispersal: Jerome Gifford reported finding lone birds in Parunuweap Canyon on July 18, 1981, and two along the Kolob Terrace Road on August 6 and 14, 1981. There are no September reports, but it can be expected at warmer mid-elevation locations, such as at the East Entrance and in the lowlands most winters. But it is most numerous during invasion years, such as the winter of 1963–64: Dennis Carter found 32 individuals along the West Rim Trail on October 3, 1963, and eight were recorded on the December 1963 CBC; none were found in 1962, 1964, or 1965. And on 25 more recent CBCs (1970–94), one or two birds were recorded only six times.

White-breasted Nuthatch. *Sitta carolinensis.*
Fairly common permanent resident; sporadic visitor in fall, winter, and spring.
Nesting birds frequent pinyon-juniper and ponderosa pine woodlands and aspen groves. I found a nest in an aspen at Lava Point on June 1, 1965, and adults were feeding young in an aspen on Carpenter Hill on June 9, 1965. Jerome Gifford recorded territorial pairs on three 40-acre breeding bird census plots: two pairs in the "slickrock ponderosa pine pinyon-juniper woodlands" (Gifford 1981) at the confluence of Pine and Clear Creeks from May 25 to July 20, 1980; one pair in the pinyon-juniper woodlands at the East

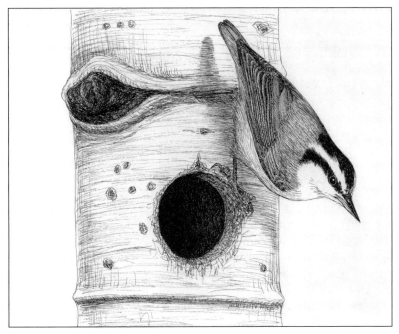

Red-breasted Nuthatch

Entrance from May 22 to July 22, 1979; and two pairs in the sparse pine-fir-aspen woodland at Lava Point from June 4 to July 24, 1978.

White-breasted Nuthatches usually move into protected side-canyons or onto the lower terraces after nestings; occasionally they move into the lower valley as early as the second week of October. These birds return to high country territories, weather permitting, by the end of January. During 25 years (1970–94) of CBCs, it was recorded 16 times, with high counts of nine and eight birds on December 27, 1985, and December 27, 1993, respectively.

Pygmy Nuthatch. *Sitta pygmaea.*
Fairly common permanent resident.

It seldom is seen away from stands of ponderosa pines, and, except when nesting, it typically occurs in flocks of a few to as many as 50 individuals (Fern Crawford reported a flock of 50 near Checkerboard Mesa on December 27, 1985). Bruce Moorhead and I found adults feeding young in ponderosa pines at three sites on Deertrap Mountain on June 22, 1965. Post-nesting birds normally remain on their ponderosa pine territories all winter; there are no records in the lowlands. And it was recorded on 12 of 25 CBCs (1970–94), including high counts of 50 and 75 individuals in December 1985 and 1986, respectively.

FAMILY CERTHIIDAE: CREEPERS

Brown Creeper. *Certhia americana.*
Rare summer resident and fairly common winter visitor.
This tiny, tree-hugging bird is probably more numerous in summer than the few records suggest. The only nesting evidence available is a juvenile seen at Potato Hollow on July 15, 1964, by Dennis Carter and Allegra Collister. One banded at the Lamoreoux Ranch on July 15, 1965, by Clyde and Lois Harden, was probably a post-nesting vagrant. The earliest lowland record is one found by Jerome Gifford at Springdale on September 3, 1979; he also found lone birds there on September 27 and October 8.

By late October it becomes more numerous in both the lowlands and at mid-elevations, such as the East Entrance area. I banded more than a dozen individuals in Oak Creek Canyon from October 24 to mid-November, and numbers increase in the lowlands through December, then begin to decline about mid-February. The latest spring record in the lowlands is one at Springdale on March 30, 1979 (Gifford). Christmas Bird Count participants missed this bird only once (on December 19, 1976) in 25 years (1970–94), and tallied high counts of 21, 32, and 24 in December 1972, 1991, and 1992, respectively.

FAMILY TROGLODYTIDAE: WRENS

Rock Wren. *Salpinctes obsoletus.*
Common summer resident and migrant; sporadic winter resident.
Summer residents are most numerous in lowland washes and on open ridges, but they occasionally occur on rocky slopes at higher

elevations. Dennis Carter found a nest, with two eggs, in Coalpits Wash on May 3, 1962; I watched adults feeding a young bird along the Watchman Trail on June 18, 1963; and Jerome Gifford recorded it in "desert shrub" communities on two breeding bird census plots in 1979: 3.5 pairs on a 60-acre plot at Grafton from May 13 to July 15, and five pairs on a 160-acre plot in Coalpits Wash from April 15 to July 2. And a more recent nesting record is one below the Canyon Overlook Trail on June 22, 1995 (V. Scheidt).

Spring migrants may arrive as early as mid-February, but Gifford reported first arrivals at Springdale on March 7, 1973, March 24, 1976, March 14, 1978, and March 30, 1980. Lowland nesters usually leave their breeding territories during the hot summers, moving into cooler canyons or onto the higher, somewhat cooler terraces. And summer birds normally begin their fall migration between mid-September and late October. However, some individuals, or more northern arrivals, may over-winter in the lowlands. Christmas Bird Count participants missed this species only three times in 25 years (1970–94), with an average of six individuals and a high count of 28 on December 17, 1973.

Canyon Wren. *Catherpes mexicanus.*
Common permanent resident.

No other bird is so representative of the Zion Park area; its wonderful descending and decelerating whistle-songs are commonplace all spring and summer and, occasionally, even on pleasant mornings in fall and winter. During May 1963, a pair built a nest in the stone wall of the Zion Inn (now the Nature Center); visitors watched the adults feeding young along the walls and rafters. I also found five fledglings in the Court of the Patriarchs on June 19, 1963, and a nest on the switchbacks below Scout's Landing on June 15, 1965. Peter Scott found a nest "along a fracture line in the ceiling of Overhang Cave" on May 28, 1974 (NPS files); Alice Galleys reported a nest in Parunuweap Canyon "in a small deep hole in the sandstone" on July 4, 1974 (NPS files). Jerome Gifford reported seven additional nests: one at the Grotto Picnic Area on August 5, 1972; one at the Watchman Campground on May 29, 1981; on three 40-acre breeding bird census plots: two in Coalpits Wash from March 31 to June 9, 1974, and again from April 28 to July 8, 1979, and one in Pine Canyon from June 12 to July 18, 1981; and finally one in Heaps' Canyon from May 14 to June 11, 1982.

Unlike the Rock Wren that utilizes similar rocky canyons and slopes, this species rarely moves out of its nesting territory and usually can be found there year-round. It was recorded on all 25 CBCs (1970–94), with an average of 17 individuals: low counts of five or fewer birds occurred only four times, and high counts of 20 or more occurred nine times; a high of 40 individuals was tallied on December 28, 1981.

Bewick's Wren. *Thryomanes bewickii.*
Common permanent resident.

This wren is partial to brushy areas in a variety of habitats, ranging from the desert to the upper limits of the pinyon-juniper woodlands, and including riparian areas in the lowlands. Nesting occurs from mid-April through July: I found a nest in a low stump at the mouth of Parunuweap Canyon on May 4, 1965; Jerome Gifford found it nesting in Springdale on May 18, 1975, at Grafton on June 10, 1979, and recorded two territorial pairs on a 160-acre breeding bird census plot in Coalpits Wash from April 15 to July 2, 1979.

There is some movement of post-nesting birds into cooler locations for the hot summer months, and some birds may leave the area altogether during severe winters. But winter populations remain reasonably stable. It was never missed on 25 CBCs (1970–94), with one to three individuals reported on four counts, 15 or more on three counts, and a high count of 35 was tallied on December 17, 1973.

House Wren. *Troglodytes aedon.*
Common summer resident; fairly common spring and rare fall migrant; sporadic winter resident.

There are several nesting records that range in elevations from the riparian woodlands in the Virgin River Valley to the high country: I found a nest under the eaves of a house in Oak Creek Canyon on June 10, 1965; nest-building in a Gambel's oak in Pine Creek Canyon on May 2, 1965; another nest in a Gambel's oak below Carpenter Hill on June 1, 1965; a nest in an aspen near Blue Springs Lake on June 9, 1965; and I banded a juvenile bird at Potato Hollow

House Wren

on August 7, 1965. Jerome Gifford found nests near the Zion Lodge and at the Grotto Picnic Area on June 22 and July 3, 1972, respectively; at Springdale on May 23, 1976; in Heaps' Canyon on May 15, 1982; and along the Narrows Trail on July 6, 1986. Summer birds may linger through August; I found one at Blue Springs Lake on August 30, 1965.

Spring migrants reach the area as early as mid-April, peak during May, and there are scattered reports through June. Fall migrants are less obvious, but there are a few reports from late August into December. Winter birds are sporadic in occurrence; it was recorded on 12 of 25 CBCs (1970–94), including counts of one to four birds on 11 years, and a high count of 18 on December 27, 1982.

Winter Wren. *Troglodytes troglodytes.*
Uncommon winter resident.

Fall reports begin as early as September 26, increase during early November, hold steady until mid-February, and then gradually decline to April 5. The majority of these are from the lowlands, especially near water, but it also has been found in winter at mid-elevations, such as at the East Entrance and in Heaps' Canyon.

And it was recorded on 15 of 25 CBCs (1970–94), including high counts of six individuals on December 28, 1981, and December 27, 1982.

There also is a single nesting record for the Zion Park area: Greer Chesher first found a singing bird along the Riverside Walk on June 3, 1982; Jack and Phyliss Wilburn next reported one half way up the trail on June 13; Peter Dring found two adults feeding three or four youngsters there on June 21; and R. J. O'Brien reported it still present on June 23.

Marsh Wren. *Cistothorus palustris.*
Uncommon migrant and winter resident.

Fall migrants have been recorded in the lowlands as early as October, and the winter residents settle in by early December; Jerome Gifford reported winter birds at the Grafton Ponds from December 11, 1983, to May 6, 1984, and from December 2, 1984, to mid-March 1985. Christmas Bird Count participants recorded it annually from 1972 to 1985, but on none of the 25 CBCs since then, which is evidence of degradation to the cattail-dominated ponds. Spring migrants are evident from early March to mid-May.

FAMILY CINCLIDAE: DIPPERS

American Dipper. *Cinclus mexicanus.*
Fairly common permanent resident.

This water-loving bird frequents fast-flowing streams year-round, although it is more often found in the upper canyons in summer and at lower elevations in winter. Nesting has been reported in May and June for Parunuweap Canyon, Pine Creek, Birch Creek, Emerald Pools, Weeping Rock, and the Narrows. I found five nests along the Narrows from Orderville Gulch to the Temple of Sinawava on May 25, 1964. Other high counts include seven individuals at the Temple of Sinawava on December 26, 1978, and again on July 7, 1979 (Jerome Gifford). And it was missed only once in 25 CBCs (1970–94), with an average of nine individuals and high counts of 22 and 24 on December 28, 1987, and December 27, 1991, respectively.

American Dipper

FAMILY MUSCICAPIDAE: MUSCICAPIDS

SUBFAMILY: SYLVIINAE: KINGLETS AND GNATCATCHERS

Golden-crowned Kinglet. *Regulus satrapa.*
Fairly common winter resident and rare spring migrant.

The earliest winter record is two individuals found by Jerome Gifford at the mouth of Parunuweap Canyon on November 5, 1978. It has not been reported again until the first week of December, but it becomes fairly common by the end of the month and through early February. The majority of these reports are from Zion Canyon, especially at Weeping Rock and along the Riverside Walk and at mid-elevation sites such as Heaps' Canyon and the East Entrance. Most of these observations are of one or a few Golden-crowned Kinglets in small flocks with chickadees, Ruby-crowned Kinglets, and Bushtits. Christmas Bird Count participants recorded Golden-crowned Kinglets on 21 of 25 years (1970–94); numbers varied from one to four individuals six years, to 20 or more tallied four years, including high counts of 41 and 40 on December 28, 1981, and December 27, 1991, respectively.

Spring migrants begin to move through the area by mid-March; Gifford recorded it at Weeping Rock on March 19 and 22 and April 2, 1982; I found it at Weeping Rock and Emerald Pools on March 31, 1965, and April 23, 1963, respectively; and Leah and Richard Foerster reported it on the Narrows Trail on April 3, 1984.

Ruby-crowned Kinglet. *Regulus calendula.*
Rare summer resident; common migrant and winter resident.

Although no nests have been found, it has been reported at pine-fir stands in the high country all summer; I found a singing pair near Blue Springs Lake on June 1, 1965; Clyde and Lois Harden banded a lone bird at the Lamoreaux Ranch on July 17, 1965; and Jerome Gifford recorded a pair in Hidden Canyon on April 24 and May 1 and 7, 1981. It is far more numerous from mid-October to early May, especially in the lowlands. Gifford recorded this Kinglet almost daily at Springdale during four winter seasons: from November 3, 1975, to April 18, 1976; September 19, 1976, to April 10, 1977;

November 7, 1977, to May 7, 1978; September 6, 1981, to April 21, 1982; and October 25, 1983, to April 3, 1984. And CBC participants recorded it every year from 1970 to 1994, including an average of 29 individuals, fewer than ten individuals only four times, and 50 or more on four occasions, including a high count of 69 on December 16, 1974.

Spring migrants pass through the area from mid-March through the first week of May. On the morning of March 27, 1965, I found dozens of Ruby-crowned Kinglets moving up-canyon near Springdale. The Hardens and I banded more than three dozen from mid-March to early May at Springdale, the Watchman orchards, and Oak Creek Canyon, compared with fewer than a dozen individuals during the fall months.

Blue-gray Gnatcatcher. *Polioptila caerulea.*
Abundant summer resident; common spring and rare fall migrant; sporadic winter visitor.

Summer residents can be found at all elevations and habitats, except at high country stands of aspen and pine-fir. There are numerous nesting records, including those recorded by Jerome Gifford on four breeding bird census plots at varied elevations: one pair in the desert shrub habitat in Coalpits Wash from April 28 to July 14, 1974, and again from April 15 to July 2, 1979; one pair in the riparian woodland at Springdale from May 23 to June 27, 1976, again from April 23 to July 10, 1978, and a late nesting pair from July 18 to August 8, 1976; one pair in mixed ponderosa pine-pinyon-juniper woodland at the confluence of Pine and Clear Creeks from May 14 to 27, 1982; and one pair in the pinyon-juniper woodland at the East Entrance from May 22 to July 22, 1979.

Fall migrants may appear in the lowlands by late August, although they are difficult to separate from post-nesting birds. Scattered records persist through September, October, November, and December, but January reports are almost nonexistent. It is possible that birds recorded on the CBCs are only late fall migrants instead of true winter populations. Christmas Bird Count participants reported it only four times in 25 years (1970–94), including one on three counts and 13 individuals on December 16, 1974; this was the earliest of the 25 December counts, and the day was colder than normal but snow-free. It has been reported only once in January and February and four times in March. Spring migrants usually appear in early April, become numerous by the middle of the month and into early May, and numbers decline by mid-May. Summer residents reach their nesting grounds by the second week of May.

SUBFAMILY TURDINAE:
SOLITAIRES, THRUSHES, AND ALLIES

Western Bluebird. *Sialia mexicana.*
Fairly common summer and winter resident; and common migrant.

This lovely bluebird, with a chestnut chest and sides, was found nesting in a dead ponderosa pine snag along the West Rim Trail on May 19, 1965 (Wauer). Jerome Gifford recorded territorial pairs on two 40-acre breeding bird census plots: four pairs in the pinyon-juniper woodland at the East Entrance from May 14 to July 15, 1978; and two pairs in the sparse pine-fir-aspen woodland at Lava Point from June 4 to July 24, 1978.

Post-nesting birds may wander into the lowlands by mid-July, but the fall migrants cannot be expected until the second week of August; numbers remain substantial until late October. Winter residents frequent open fields and hillsides in the lowlands, and on mild winter days they can be reasonably common at mid-elevations; I found it "common" at the East Entrance on November 7, 1953, and "several flocks" there on January 18, 1963. It was missed only four times in 25 (1970–94) CBCs, with a high count of 46 individuals on December 29, 1986. Spring migrants reach the Zion Park area in late February; they are most numerous in the lowlands until mid-March, and at higher elevations until mid-April. However, cold fronts at this time of year may force birds back into lower elevations for a few to several days.

Mountain Bluebird. *Sialia currucoides.*
Uncommon summer resident; fairly common migrant; sporadic winter resident.

This is the sky-blue bird of the high country fields and meadows. Clyde and Lois Harden and I found a nest in an aspen on Carpenter

Townsend's Solitaire

Hill on June 9, 1965, and Bruce Moorhead and I found another nest in a ponderosa pine on Deertrap Mountain on June 22, 1965. Post-nesting birds spend the summer months in the high country. They usually are common along the Kolob Terrace Road from late June to mid-October: Hardens banded birds at the Lamoreaux Ranch on July 17 and 18, 1965; Jerome Gifford reported 66 individuals on the "Upper Kolob" (Gifford 1987) on October 14, 1983; and I found hundreds in the open fields from Cave Valley to the Kolob Reservoir on October 2, 1995.

Winter residents or visitors are rather sporadic in occurrence. Christmas Bird Count participants recorded it only 10 times in 25 years (1970–94), with one to five individuals on six years and much higher numbers on December 27, 1985 (51), December 27, 1988 (50), December 27, 1989 (37), and an all-time high of 138 on December 27, 1994. A similar pattern was recorded in 1962, 1963, and 1964, when 29 birds were found in 1962 and none in 1963 and 1964. Spring migrants may put in their appearance by mid-February and be evident until mid-May. These birds are most numerous during storms, when flocks congregate at lower, more protected sites: I found more than 200 individuals at the ZCVC during a snowstorm on May 5, 1964, and Gifford reported 60 there on May 14, 1977.

Townsend's Solitaire. *Myadestes townsendi.*
Uncommon summer resident; common migrant; fairly common winter resident.

Nesting was documented by Jerome Gifford, who reported three pairs of Townsend's Solitaires on a 40-acre breeding bird census plot at Lava Point from June 4 to July 24, 1978. Post-nesting or early migrants have been found in the lowlands as early as August 22, numbers increase by mid-September, and winter populations or spring migrants can usually be found until mid-April. Gifford reported late birds at Springdale on May 3 and 5, 1973, and May 21, 1975. Migrants can be expected at all elevations.

Winter birds are most numerous in the lowlands and at mid-elevations, such as the East Entrance. It also is somewhat sporadic in occurrence; during the winter of 1963–64 and the following spring it was abundant in the Virgin River Valley, with records through the first week of May; 29 were seen on the 1963 CBC, in contrast to only one in 1962 and 10 in 1964. On more recent CBCs, participants missed it only once in 25 years (1970–94), with an average count of 10, and high counts of 22, 21, and 24 on December 27, 1982, December 27, 1989, and December 27, 1994, respectively.

Swainson's Thrush. *Catharus ustulatus.*
Casual migrant.

The first record for the park and the entire Virgin River Valley is a female collected in Oak Creek Canyon on May 27, 1966; it was racially identified by Lester L. Short as *swainsonii* (northern Utah nester) (Wauer 1969). It was next reported in Coalpits Wash where Peter Scott discovered four individuals on March 26, 1974; one was still there the next day. Jerome Gifford found one at Springdale on May 11, 1977, and one at Rockville on October 13, 1980.

Hermit Thrush. *Catharus guttatus.*
Common summer resident; uncommon migrant and winter resident.

Clyde and Lois Harden found a nest, containing four eggs, at Blue Springs Lake on June 19, 1965, and Jerome Gifford recorded territorial pairs on two breeding bird census plots: one pair in the 40-acre pine-fir-aspen woodland at Lava Point from June 4 to July 24, 1978, and one pair in the 50-acre "deciduous-coniferous north slope" (Gifford 1979a) habitat in Heaps' Canyon from June 17 to July 16, 1983.

Post-nesting and/or early fall migrants may appear in the lowlands as early as late August, there are a few scattered reports in September and October, and numbers increase considerably during November; I banded more than a dozen individuals in Oak Creek Canyon from November 3 to December 11. Winter birds can usually be found on the Virgin River floodplain as well as in various side-canyons and on the mid-elevation terraces, at least during mild weather. On 25 CBCs (1970–94), it was missed only five times: counts averaged four individuals, and high counts of 17 and 11 were tallied on December 27, 1988, and December 27, 1993, respectively. Also of interest, a lone bird was recorded on only one of three CBCs in 1962, 1963, and 1964, and lone birds were found on only two CBCs from 1970 to 1976; but it was reported every year since then, suggesting an increase in winter populations.

Wintering birds remain fairly stable through early February, after which there is an obvious decline in numbers until mid-April, which is when scattered spring migrants appear at all elevations. The spring movement lasts until mid-May.

American Robin. *Turdus migratorius.*
Common summer resident, migrant, and winter resident.

This well-known red-breasted thrush can be found year-round at almost all elevations; exceptions include the desert in summer and the extreme high country in winter. And during the nesting season they are one of the area's most vocal songbirds. There are numerous nesting records from late April to mid-August. I found a nest, containing four eggs, 3.5 feet high on a white fir near Blue Springs Lake on June 1, 1965, and a second nest there, containing two eggs and two nestlings, seven feet high on a white fir on June 9, 1965. Jerome Gifford recorded a high of 17 territorial pairs on one 25-acre breeding bird census plot in the Watchman Campground in 1986. Gifford also recorded seven pairs on a 60-acre plot, dominated by apple orchards and pastures, at Grafton in 1979, and two pairs on a 40-acre plot in sparse pine-fir-aspen woodland at Lava Point in 1978.

Post-nesting birds in the lowlands often move onto the higher, cooler terraces, where they may remain until cooler weather forces them back into the lowlands or to migrate out of the area entirely. Migrants are obvious in the lowlands by the end of October, and numbers normally increase during December. Some years, especially those with more than average snowfall, lowland populations are extensive. Gifford reported that during a January 1978 storm, hundreds of Robins moved into Zion Canyon and along the Virgin River from the northeast; they remained for about three weeks, then departed in the direction they had come. During 25 years (1970–94) of CBCs, the highest count (722) corresponded to the deepest snowfall and one of the coldest count days, December 27, 1988. Average CBC numbers (122) generally correspond to moderate weather conditions.

Stormy conditions also can fill the canyons during the spring migration. I found 150 individuals at the ZCVC during a snowstorm on May 5, 1964, and Gifford recorded 800 and 500 individuals at Springdale during a storm on April 16 and 17, 1976, respectively.

FAMILY MIMIDAE:
MOCKINGBIRDS, THRASHERS, AND ALLIES

Northern Mockingbird. *Mimus polyglottos.*
Uncommon summer resident and casual winter resident.

This bird normally does not arrive in the Zion Park area until the second week of May. The vast majority of reports are from arid lowland washes, but Jerome Gifford found lone birds at the East Entrance on May 13, 1964, and May 31, 1984. Nesting usually is well underway by early June. Clifford Presnall found three singing, territorial males near the South Entrance from May 14 to June 10, 1934 (Presnall 1935); a pair nested successfully in a sagebrush near the East Entrance in June 1963 (NPS files); and Gifford found territorial birds on two breeding bird census plots: one pair was recorded on a 26-acre plot—dominated by ponds, riparian vegetation, and fields—at Springdale from June 4 to July 24, 1976, and another pair was present on a 60-acre plot—dominated by orchards and pastures—at Grafton from May 13 to July 15, 1979. Post-nesting birds apparently move out of the area, as records are scarce during August, September and October. And winter sightings are limited to the open slopes in the lower canyons, especially in the Rockville area, where Gifford photographed one on January 15 and 18, 1975. It has been reported on CBCs only once (December 28, 1981) in 25 years (1970–94).

Sage Thrasher. *Oreoscoptes montanus.*
Casual migrant.

Spring records range from April 1 to May 17: I found two individuals in Coalpits Wash on April 11, 1963, and another near Rockville two days later; one was found at Zion on April 1, 1975 (Kingery 1975); and Jerome Gifford reported one at Springdale on May 17, 1984. Fall reports are limited to two sightings: Dennis Carter and I found one near the ZCVC on September 22, 1964, and Gifford reported one in Coalpits Wash on November 29, 1981.

Brown Thrasher. *Toxostoma rufum.*
Two records.

The first report is of one trapped by Henry Grantham while banding birds in Zion Canyon on December 6, 1935; it was collected the next day and prepared as a study skin, representing the first Utah record (Grantham 1936). A second Brown Thrasher was reported for the same locality by Clifford Presnall in late March 1936 (NPS files).

FAMILY MOTACILLIDAE: WAGTAILS AND PIPITS

American Pipit. *Anthus rubescens.*
Fairly common migrant and winter visitor.

Records extend from October 2, through the winter months, to May 1; there is one earlier report at the Grafton Ponds by Jerome Gifford on September 18, 1983. The majority of the reports are from the lowlands, especially on open, flooded fields along the Virgin River; Gifford found it at Grafton almost daily from October 12, 1982, to May 1, 1983. There also are two high country records: I found a small flock along the Kolob Terrace Road on December 6, 1965, and more than 40 individuals along the shore of the Kolob Reservoir on October 2, 1995. And Karen and Harvey Swainse found two "below the Narrows" (NPS files) on November 25, 1995. Christmas Bird Count participants recorded it on 18 of 25 years (1970–94), including more than 50 individuals on five counts and a high count of 79 on December 27, 1989. Gifford also reported high counts of 80 on January 18, 1980, 93 on March 12, 1982, and 54 on March 19, 1983, all at Grafton.

FAMILY BOMBYCILLIDAE: WAXWINGS

Bohemian Waxwing. *Bombycilla garrulus.*
Sporadic winter visitor.

This northern songbird occurs only during invasion years, when large flocks appear briefly during the winter months. The first record is a flock of 55 individuals found above Maloney Hill on December 20, 1963 (Wauer). Jerome Gifford next found 59 at Springdale on December 27, 1968, 32 birds at Springdale on May 25, 1974, and 38 near the mouth of Zion Canyon on November 13, 1980. The highest number reported was 150 in Springdale on the December 27, 1968, CBC (Barbara Lund).

Cedar Waxwing. *Bombycilla cedrorum.*
Fairly common fall, winter, and spring visitor.

Records extend from September 21, through the winter months, to June 15. It can appear in pairs or in huge flocks that move into suitable feeding areas for a few to several days and then move elsewhere; almost any fruit or berry will suffice. A high of 200 individuals was reported by Jerome Gifford at Rockville on November 21, 1984. And CBC participants recorded it on 10 of 25 years (1970–94), including a high count of 162 on December 27, 1990. Spring birds may linger surprisingly late into the nesting season before leaving.

FAMILY PTILOGONATIDAE: SILKY-FLYCATCHERS

Phainopepla. *Phainopepla nitens.*
Uncommon summer resident.

Records of this crested songbird extend from April 22 to September 20, and there is one very late November 23, 1983, report for Springdale (Jerome Gifford). Except for one found in Oak Creek Canyon on May 20, 1983 (Gifford), and another one there on September 11,

Phainopepla

1973 (Jim Haycock), all reports are from the Virgin River Valley below the South Entrance. Gifford recorded arrival and departure dates at Springdale during five seasons: from May 22 to July 19, 1981; May 22 to July 31, 1982; June 5 to August 28, 1983; May 21 to June 28, 1985; and May 1 to July 11, 1986. He also recorded nesting pairs on two breeding bird census plots: one pair on a 26-acre plot—dominated by riparian woodlands and ponds—at Springdale from April 23 to July 10, 1978; and 4.5 pairs on a 60-acre plot—dominated by orchards and pastures—at Grafton from May 13 to July 15, 1979. Post-nesting birds move elsewhere soon after nesting; there are only a handful of reports in August and September.

FAMILY LANIIDAE: SHRIKES

Northern Shrike. *Lanius excubitor.*
Sporadic winter visitor.
This northern predator is present in southern Utah only during invasion years. One was banded near the South Entrance on March 7, 1933, and seen several times during the winter by Henry Grantham

(Presnall 1935). It was not reported again until the winter of 1964–65, when three were recorded on the December 29 CBC (Wauer). Since then, it has been reported on only five of 25 (1970–94) CBCs: in December 1977, 1978, 1980, 1988, and 1989. Although the majority of the reports are from the lowlands, Jerome Gifford also reported birds at Clear Creek, Hepworth Wash, and near the East Entrance.

Loggerhead Shrike. *Lanius ludovicianus.*
Rare migrant and winter resident.

The status of this Shrike has declined during the last 50 years: Clifford Presnall considered it "fairly common in summer" (Presnall 1935); by the 1960s, it was an "uncommon summer resident in the pinyon-juniper woodland, a fairly common migrant below the highlands, and a fairly common winter resident in the lowlands" (Wauer and Carter 1965); since then there have been only about a dozen scattered reports. While CBC participants tallied four birds in 1962 and 1963, and one in 1965, one or two individuals were recorded on only seven of 25 CBCs between 1970 and 1994.

FAMILY STURNIDAE: STARLINGS

European Starling. *Sturnus vulgaris.*
Abundant permanent resident.

This non-native bird is present only in the lowlands and most generally in the towns and farming areas along the Virgin River. The first report in the Zion Park area was in November 1955 (Carl Jepson), but reports increased dramatically afterward; CBC participants recorded 447 individuals in 1962 and 1,153 in 1963. And from 1970 to 1994, count totals ranged from a low of 12 individuals to more than 1,000 on five counts, including a high of 2,624 on December 28, 1987.

Nesting birds utilize crevices in trees—oftentimes in prime riparian woodlands—as well as in old buildings and on cliffs, usurping nest sites of other cavity-nesters such as woodpeckers, Ash-throated Flycatchers, chickadees, Plain Titmice, and Western Bluebirds.

Starlings appear in great flocks, completely dominating feeding sites in fields and pastures. Jerome Gifford reported "migrating" (Gifford 1987) flocks of 1,500 individuals at Grafton on April 23, 1980, 3,500 there on November 13, 1981, and 5,600 there on November 27, 1982.

FAMILY VIREONIDAE: VIREOS

Bell's Vireo. *Vireo bellii.*
Casual summer resident.

Records extend from April 16 to August 26. The Virgin River Valley lies at the northwestern edge of its range, and nesting records in the Zion Park area are scarce. Dennis Carter found a nest at the mouth of Parunuweap Canyon on August 17, 1962, and observed an immature bird begging food from an adult nine days later. Jerome Gifford recorded one territorial pair on a 60-acre breeding bird census plot—dominated by riparian woodland, orchards, and pastures—at Grafton (at the mouth of Parunuweap Canyon) from May 13 to July 15, 1979. And Allan R. Keith found one individual (from nearby Grafton?) between Springdale and Rockville on August 8, 1979.

Gray Vireo. *Vireo vicinior.*
Fairly common summer resident.

Records range from April 20 to August 21, and there is also a lone September report: Jerome Gifford found one along the West Rim Trail on September 12, 1980. It is most numerous from early May through July, and nesting has been recorded on several occasions: I found two adults nest-building on a Gambel's oak in Taylor Creek on May 21, 1964; two immature birds were banded in Oak Creek Canyon on July 9, 1963, as was a territorial pair on Firepit Knoll on June 1, 1965; Michael Hays reported a nest in lower Emerald Pools Canyon on June 2, 1970; and Gifford reported one or two territorial pairs on six breeding bird census plots: in desert shrub habitat in lower Parunuweap Canyon from June 1 to July 20, 1980, and also May 3 to July 16, 1982; in the pinyon-juniper woodland near the South Entrance from May 14 to July 15, 1978; on the riparian-scrub oak slopes near the Temple of Sinawava from May 28 to July 14,

Solitary Vireo

1983, and May 11 to June 29, 1986; in the mixed ponderosa pine-pinyon-juniper woodland at the confluence on Pine and Creek creeks from May 25 to July 20, 1980; in the mixed "deciduous-coniferous north slope" (Gifford 1984a) habitat in Heaps' Canyon from May 27 to July 9, 1983; and in the pinyon-juniper woodland at the East Entrance from May 14 to 15, 1979, and from May 30 to July 22, 1979.

Although this little, nondescript songbird is not often seen, its presence can usually be detected on its nesting grounds by the male's constant singing: three whistle-notes at a moderate, high, then lower scale, respectively, repeated over and over again.

Solitary Vireo. *Vireo solitarius.*
Common summer resident and migrant.

This is one of the park's most wide-ranging songbirds and is present at all elevations and habitats, except in the arid desert. Records extend from April 3 to early September, and arrival and departure dates at Springdale were documented by Jerome Gifford: from April 25 to September 5, 1979, April 25 to September 2, 1980, and April

23 to September 4, 1985. And there are numerous records of nesting: I found a nest in the Court of the Patriarchs on May 18, 1965; one along the Narrows Trail on May 18, 1965; and a nest, containing nestlings, on a boxelder on Bridge Mountain on June 12, 1966; and Greer Chesher found a nest in Oak Creek Canyon on May 25, 1981. Jerome Gifford documented territorial pairs on four breeding bird census plots: in the riparian woodland in Coalpits Wash from April 29 to July 8, 1979; in the Watchman Campground from May 22 to June 27, 1986; near the Temple of Sinawava from May 22 to July 14, 1983; a high of eight territorial pairs was found on a 50-acre plot in the "deciduous-coniferous north slope" (Gifford 1983d) habitat in Heaps' Canyon from April 24 to July 17, 1982; and pairs were also found in the pinyon-juniper woodland at the East Entrance from May 22 to July 22, 1979.

Post-nesting birds generally remain on their breeding territories, at least until late July, after which there is a wide-spread exodus. Most of the migrants remain on the high terraces and seldom appear in the lowlands. However, there are scattered fall reports in the lowlands from August to mid-September, fewer to mid-November, and one very late sighting at Springdale on December 4, 1973 (Gifford).

Warbling Vireo. *Vireo gilvus.*
Common summer resident and migrant.

Records of this loud songster extend from April 17 to September 7, but it is most numerous from May to mid-July. Nesting birds frequent broadleaf habitats from the riparian woodlands along the Virgin River and side-canyons up to the aspen groves in the high country. It is especially numerous in Zion Canyon and at Potato Hollow. Jerome Gifford recorded territorial pairs on four breeding bird census plots: in Springdale from May 23 to August 8, 1976; in the Watchman Campground from June 7 to August 11, 1981, and again from May 6 to July 15, 1982; near the Temple of Sinawava from May 28 to July 14, 1983; and in Heaps' Canyon from May 1 to July 16, 1983. This vireo may share territories with Solitary Vireos, with the Solitary nesting in the lower tree branches and the Warbling Vireo using the upper portions of the tree.

Post-nesting and fall migrants can be found from mid-July through early September; Clyde and Lois Harden banded birds at the Lamoreaux Ranch on July 17 and 27, 1965, and there are scattered reports for high-country sites to mid-August and in the lowlands to September 7. Spring migrants reach the lower canyons by mid-April, and they are most numerous by the end of the month and during the first half of May.

FAMILY EMBERIZIDAE: EMBERIZIDS

SUBFAMILY PARULINAE: WOOD-WARBLERS

Orange-crowned Warbler. *Vermivora celata.*
Fairly common summer resident and migrant.

Summer residents are limited to the aspen groves and brush-covered slopes in the high country. Dennis Carter and Bruce Moorhead observed an adult feeding an immature bird in Potato Hollow on June 29, 1963, and I found a territorial pair in the aspens near Blue Springs Lake on June 1, 1965. Post-nesting birds and/or fall migrants may appear in the lowlands by mid-August, and there are scattered reports to the end of October.

The earliest of the spring migrants was recorded on March 25 (one by Jerome Gifford at Springdale in 1983), but they normally do not reach the Zion Park area until mid-April. Numbers greatly increase during the first two weeks of May, and there is a secondary movement in late May; banding records in Oak Creek Canyon range between May 3 and 13, and again from May 24 to 27 (Wauer). There are no further reports in the lowlands until August, with the exception of two birds reported at Rockville on June 18, 1979 (Louise Excell). And there also is a single winter record: Gifford found one at the Springdale Ponds on January 19, 1980.

Nashville Warbler. *Vermivora ruficapilla.*
Casual migrant.

Spring records extend from April 12 to May 26, all from Springdale by Jerome Gifford. Fall reports are limited to lone birds found in the Watchman Campground on September 12 and 20, 1963 (Dennis Carter). Gifford reported birds at Springdale on September 15, 1974, and November 2, 1983, and a very late migrant in the Watchman Campground on December 4, 1983.

Virginia's Warbler

Virginia's Warbler. *Vermivora virginiae.*
Common summer resident and spring migrant; casual fall migrant.

The first spring migrants appear in the lower canyons the first week of April and numbers peak in early May, when it can be the single most common migrating warbler; I banded more than two dozen individuals at Springdale and in Oak Creek Canyon from April 20 to May 14.

Nesting is well underway by the end of April. Breeding birds are pretty well restricted to stands of Gambel's oak that are scattered throughout the pinyon-juniper woodlands and on warmer slopes and the valleys at higher elevations. On May 19, 1965, I counted 23 individuals along the West Rim Trail, from Refrigerator Canyon to the Great West Canyon Overlook. I also found adults feeding young at Potato Hollow on June 27, 1963; Shane Pruett reported a territorial pair in Oak Creek Canyon on April 9, 1993; and Jerome Gifford recorded nesting birds on two breeding bird census plots: in the "deciduous-coniferous-north slope" (Gifford 1983d) habitat in Heaps' Canyon from May 7 to July 17, 1982, and again from May 7 to July 16, 1983; and on the riparian-shrub oak slopes near the Temple of Sinawava from May 4 to July 6, 1986.

Post-nesting birds and fall migrants remain on the upper terraces until at least mid-August. The first lowland sightings occur in mid-September, and there are widely scattered reports to early December. The latest record is a lone bird found at Springdale on December 3 and 4, 1973 (Gifford).

Lucy's Warbler. *Vermivora luciae.*
Fairly common summer resident.

This little warbler occurs only in the riparian woodlands and adjacent mesquites in the Virgin River Valley, where it is at the northern edge of its range. Records extend from March 29 (I found one at the mouth of Parunuweap Canyon in 1965) to August 12 (Jerome Gifford reported one at Springdale in 1976). It can easily be overlooked because of its dull coloration and habit of feeding high in cottonwoods, but territorial birds sing a melodic, trilling song. Gifford found a nesting pair in the Watchman Campground on May 20, 1982, and territorial pairs on two breeding bird census plots: one pair on a 26-acre plot—dominated by riparian vegetation and ponds—at Springdale from April 23 to July 10, 1978, and two pairs on a 60-acre plot—dominated by riparian vegetation, orchards, and pastures—at Grafton from May 13 to July 15, 1979.

Yellow Warbler. *Dendroica petechia.*
Fairly common summer resident and common migrant.

This little songster resides in riparian woodlands in the lowlands and willow thickets in the high country. I found two territorial males at Blue Springs Lake on June 1, 1965, and an adult feeding young in Parunuweap Canyon on June 13, 1965. And Jerome Gifford recorded territorial pairs on five breeding bird census plots: two pairs at Grafton from May 13 to July 10, 1979; five pairs at Springdale from April 23 to July 10, 1978, including one nest with two Brown-headed Cowbird nestlings; two pairs in the Watchman Campground from May 20 to July 15, 1983; one pair near the Temple of Sinawava from May 11 to July 6, 1986; and one pair in Heaps' Canyon from June 17 to July 1, 1983.

Post-nesting birds and early migrants have been reported in the high country to mid-August, and in the lowlands to September 24. The earliest spring migrant may arrive in the lower canyons the first week of April (Kevin Wallace reported one male at Rockville on April 6, 1985), but they normally do not arrive until later in the month; Gifford recorded first arrivals on April 17, 1975, April 23, 1978 and 1985, and May 16, 1976. Spring migrants are most numerous from May 10 to 25; Hardens and I banded 18 individuals at Springdale and in Oak Creek Canyon during this period in 1965. And there also is one winter record: a first-year male came daily to a Springdale feeder from January 12 to March 1, 1974 (Clyde and Lois Harden).

Yellow-rumped Warbler. *Dendroica coronata.*
Fairly common summer resident; common migrant; fairly common in winter.

Both the eastern "Myrtle Warbler" and the western "Audubon's Warbler" occur in the Zion Park area, and sightings were maintained separately until the two were lumped together by the AOU. Therefore, they will be discussed separately. Typical male Audubon's Warblers possess a yellow throat and a large, white wing patch, whereas typical Myrtle Warblers have a white throat and two distinct white wing bars.

Yellow-rumped (Audubon's) Warbler

Myrtle Warblers are rare spring migrants from April 8 to May 20; I banded three individuals at Springdale on April 19, 20, and 21, 1965. And there also is one winter report: one came to a Springdale feeder daily from January 11 to 27, 1974 (Clyde and Lois Harden).

Audubon's Warblers have been recorded every month, but they are most numerous in spring from mid-April to mid-May, when thousands of birds migrate through the canyons. Clyde and Lois Harden and I banded 407 individuals at the Springdale Ponds between April 10 and May 15, 1965. And Jerome Gifford reported an estimated 200 birds migrating past one Springdale motel on May 3, 1975. Nesting birds utilize conifers in the high country: Clifford Presnall found young just off the nest in Potato Hollow on July 1, 1934 (Presnall 1935); nest-building was observed at Blue Springs Lake on June 9, 1965, and a second nest with eggs was found there on June 22, 1965 (Wauer and Hardens); and Gifford recorded territorial pairs on two breeding bird census plots: one pair on a 50-acre plot, within a "deciduous-coniferous-northslope" (Gifford 1983d) habitat, in Heaps' Canyon from April 24 to May 7, 1982; and one pair on a

40-acre plot—dominated by a sparse pine-fir-aspen woodland—at Lava Point from June 4 to July 24, 1978.

There is an almost immediate departure of post-nesting birds, and reports from mid-July to mid-September are scarce. However, fall migrants may appear in the lowlands by mid-September and become more numerous in October. Gifford recorded arrival and departure dates at Springdale and Grafton during five winter seasons: from October 16, 1974, to February 19, 1975; December 18, 1976, to May 1, 1977; October 30, 1979, to April 29, 1980; October 26, 1980, to April 14, 1981; and October 4, 1983, to May 1, 1984. And CBC participants missed it only once (1972) in 25 years (1970–94), with high counts of 25 or more birds in December 1983 (29), 1984 (28), 1992 (58), and 1993 (37).

Black-throated Gray Warbler. *Dendroica nigrescens.*
Common summer resident.

Records extend from April 3 to August 17, and nesting birds are pretty well restricted to the pinyon-juniper woodlands. I banded two immature birds in Oak Creek Canyon on July 16 and 17, 1964. Jerome Gifford recorded territorial pairs on four 40-acre breeding bird census plots: one pair near the Temple of Sinawava from May 25 to July 6, 1976, and May 22 to July 14, 1983; six pairs at the confluence of Pine and Clear Creeks from May 31 to July 18, 1982; a high of eight territorial pairs in Heaps' Canyon from April 24 to July 17, 1982, and five pairs there from May 7 to July 16, 1983; and five territorial pairs at the East Entrance from June 15 to July 31, 1977, and May 14 to July 15, 1978.

Post-nesting birds leave immediately after their young are fledged; fall records are scarce, but include 10 individuals found in the Kolob Canyons on August 6, 1994 (Steve Summers); Clyde and Lois Harden banded one at the Lamoreaux Ranch on August 8, 1965; I banded one in Oak Creek Canyon on August 17, 1965; there are no September reports; and Gifford reported four and eight individuals at Springdale on October 17 and 18, 1974, respectively, one on October 24, 1975, and one on October 3, 1983.

Although this black-and-white warbler, with a tiny yellow patch in front of each eye, can be difficult to find when nesting, its very distinct song—four or more notes, like "swee, swee, ker-swee, sick" or "wee-zy, wee-zy, wee-zy, we-zy, weet," with the last syllable either ascending or descending—can help to locate this lovely bird.

Grace's Warbler. *Dendroica graciae.*
Fairly common summer resident; rare migrant.

Records extend from April 23 to August 14, but it can be expected during the nesting season only at stands of ponderosa pines at mid-elevations. During the summers of 1964 and 1965, I found it on a few occasions among the open ponderosa pines in the vicinity of the East Entrance, Checkerboard Mesa, Hepworth Wash, Deertrap Mountain, and Bridge Mountain; and Jerome Gifford recorded two territorial pairs on a 40-acre breeding bird census plot at the confluence of Pine and Clear Creeks from June 20 to July 8, 1982.

Spring migrants have been reported in the lowlands during the last ten days in April, and fall migrants have been reported only in the high country: I found one above Cave Valley on July 25, 1965; Gifford reported one from the East Entrance on August 6, 1986, and Steve and Priscilla Summers found one on Pocket Mesa on August 14, 1995.

American Redstart. *Setophaga ruticilla.*
Five records.

The first reports include a female or immature bird at the mouth of Parunuweap Canyon on June 4, 1963 (Dennis Carter), and I found an adult male at Rockville the very next day. It was not reported again until Jerome Gifford discovered a female at Springdale on November 15, 1972, and a male at Springdale on August 11, 1978. Steve Hedges reported an adult male near the ZCVC on May 19, 1979. In addition, a male collected in Beaver Dam Wash (below St. George) on May 18, 1963, represented the first specimen for the Virgin River Valley (Wauer 1969).

Northern Waterthrush. *Seiurus noveboracensis.*
Casual spring migrant.

Records extend from a very early spring report at Grafton on March 26 (by Jerome Gifford in 1976) to May 21. I recorded one at the Springdale Ponds on May 13, 1965; one of three seen at Springdale was banded (Clyde and Lois Harden) and another was collected

MacGillivray's Warbler

(Wauer) on May 15, 1965; and Gifford found one at Springdale on May 21, 1976. There also is a single fall report: one bird along the Riverside Walk on September 22, 1940, which represents the first park sighting (Russell Grater).

MacGillivray's Warbler. *Oporornis tolmiei.*
Uncommon summer resident; fairly common spring and casual fall migrant.

This bird resides in summer only at thickets near water areas in the high country. I found singing males in the willows at Blue Springs Lake on June 1 and 9, 1965. It is most numerous as a spring migrant: Jerome Gifford reported it at Springdale on April 6 and 27, 1983, but it is far more numerous from May 3 to 19, during which time Clyde and Lois Harden and I banded 16 individuals at Springdale and in Oak Creek Canyon in 1965, and two additional birds were banded there on May 24 and June 2, 1966. There also is a June 27, 1965, sighting at Lava Point (Wauer); there are no reports in July; and there are a few widely scattered reports from the lowlands from August 15 to October 22.

Common Yellowthroat. *Geothlypis trichas.*
Casual summer resident and uncommon spring migrant.

Records of this wetland warbler extend from April 23 (one at the
Grafton Ponds by Ella Sorensen in 1985) to August 30. The major-
ity of these are from Springdale during the first two weeks in May;
Clyde and Lois Harden and I banded six individuals there in 1965.
And in 1976, Jerome Gifford recorded two territorial pairs on a
breeding bird census plot at Springdale from May 23 to August 1.
Except for a sighting of one bird in Pine Canyon on May 4, 1965
(Wauer), all reports are from the lowlands.

Wilson's Warbler. *Wilsonia pusilla.*
Fairly common spring and rare fall migrant.

Spring migrants move through the lower canyons from May 2–26,
and 12 individuals were banded in Springdale and Oak Creek
Canyon from May 6–24 (Wauer). A high spring count of eight
individuals was recorded at Grafton on May 20, 1983 (Jerome
Gifford). Fall migration is scattered out over a much longer period,
from July 23 to November 2, and birds are never as numerous as
they are in spring. There also are two winter reports: one was
recorded on the December 12, 1983, CBC (Gifford); and Catherine
Inman reported two from the Watchman Residential Area on February 20, 1983.

Painted Redstart. *Myioborus pictus.*
Casual spring visitor.

The first record for Zion Park and Utah was one found in Heaps'
Canyon by Vasco Tanner on April 26, 1930 (Presnall 1935). It was
not reported again until Robert Hudson discovered one in Emerald
Pools Canyon on April 22, 1966; I found three individuals there two
days later, and Dick Russell found one still present there on April 30
(Wauer 1969). It was next reported by Leah and Richard Foerster at
Weeping Rock on April 28, 1975, and Ken Kertell and Peter Scott
observed it there on May 1 and 2. And finally, Phil Brouse reported
a displaying male in Imlay Canyon on April 20, 1994. These records
probably represent spring migrants that overshot their normal
breeding grounds in central and west-central Arizona, although it
has recently been found breeding on the west slope of the Beaver

Yellow-breasted Chat

Dam Mountains (Don Haney, manuscript submitted to *Utah Birds*, 1996).

Yellow-breasted Chat. *Icteria virens.*
Rare summer resident and fairly common spring migrant.

Records extend from May 2 to July 30, and there are two fall reports: I observed one at Springdale on August 13, 1964, and banded one in Oak Creek Canyon on September 16, 1963. Except for one found at the East Entrance on June 2, 1964 (Jerome Gifford), all reports are from the lowlands.

The breeding status of this large warbler has declined in the last 25 years, according to Gifford. It was once considered a "common summer resident in brushy areas in the Virgin River Valley" (Wauer and Carter 1965). Gifford found territorial pairs on breeding bird census plots in both Coalpits Wash and at the Springdale Ponds in 1974 and 1976, but he could not find it during six consecutive nesting seasons after 1981. And the only later report is that of Shane Pruett, who "heard an individual singing almost daily and saw it occasionally during May and early June [1995] in a willow thicket" (NPS files) below Rockville.

SUBFAMILY THRAUPINAE: TANAGERS

Summer Tanager. *Piranga rubra.*
Rare summer resident.

Records extend from May 2 (a pair seen at Rockville by Kevin Wallace in 1985) to October 7, when a lone male was found at Springdale on October 5 and 7, 1995 (Wauer and Mary Hunnicutt). This lovely bird has nested in the Zion Park area only since the 1970s; Jerome Gifford found the first nest on a pecan tree at Grafton on July 17, 1978 (it also was seen by Louise Excell on July 19). Since then, it has nested annually in the riparian woodland along the Virgin River. It had been a summer resident in the lower Virgin River Valley at Santa Clara and St. George at least since the 1950s (Wauer and Russell 1967).

Western Tanager. *Piranga ludoviciana.*
Fairly common summer resident and common migrant.

The earliest spring report is a male found on Angel's Landing on April 6, 1984, by Jill Blumenthal. But it usually does not appear until late April, and migrants can be numerous from early May to early June, when it may be the most conspicuous bird in Zion Canyon. Jerome Gifford found 30 individuals at the Grotto Picnic Area on May 22, 1973.

Nesting occurs at all elevations, although it is most numerous at mid-elevations and the high country. I found a pair at Cave Valley on June 1, 1965, and a copulating pair at Blue Springs Lake on June 9, 1965. Gifford recorded territorial pairs on four breeding bird census plots: in the Watchman Campground from May 14 to 20, 1983, and May 22 to 29, 1986; Heaps' Canyon from June 4 to July 17, 1982, and May 21 to July 16, 1983; near the Temple of Sinawava on May 22, 1983; and at the East Entrance from May 14 to 28, 1978.

Post-nesting birds may wander throughout the high country, and a few move into the lower canyons by early August; numbers increase substantially through mid-September, after which there are only scattered reports until October 10. And Gifford reported that in early July 1979, Western Tanagers "attacked my hummingbird feeders and stripped an early peach tree (along with orioles)" (Gifford 1987) in Springdale.

SUBFAMILY CARDINALINAE:
CARDINALS, GROSBEAKS, AND ALLIES

Rose-breasted Grosbeak. *Pheucticus ludovicianus.*
Casual spring visitor.

Records extend only from April 27 to June 28. The first area record was a male captured in a mist net at the Springdale Ponds on May 3, 1965; it was collected and the specimen represents the first for Utah (Wauer and Russell 1967). The next report was a male that hit a window at the L. D. Excell home in Springdale on May 21, 1975; it was identified and released by Glen Arnold. Also in 1975, two adults visited Jerome Gifford's Springdale feeders on June 2 to 4 and June 3 to 5. And there are five additional reports: Robert Clark observed a male in Springdale on May 27, 1976; Gifford found one there on June 28, 1980; Shane Pruett found a male in Oak Creek Canyon on June 26, 1993; Jim and Shirley Thielen reported one in the South Campground on April 27, 1993; and Sheri Fedorchak found a male in the Watchman Residential Area on June 28, 1995.

Black-headed Grosbeak. *Pheucticus melanocephalus.*
Common summer resident and spring migrant; rare in fall.

This is one of Zion Canyon's most numerous and obvious songbirds in summer; it resides in riparian woodlands and pinyon-juniper-oak communities at all elevations. There are numerous records of nesting, including those recorded by Jerome Gifford on five breeding bird census plots: two pairs on a 160-acre plot in Coalpits Wash from April 15 to July 2, 1979; four pairs on a 60-acre plot at Grafton from May 13 to July 15, 1979; three pairs on a 26-acre plot at Springdale from April 23 to July 10, 1978; three pairs on a 40-acre plot near the Temple of Sinawava from May 11 to July 6, 1986; and one pair in a 40-acre plot at the East Entrance from June 5 to July 8, 1978.

Blue Grosbeak

Although Gifford found it at Springdale as early as April 7, his other arrival and departure reports extended from April 25 to August 25, 1979; April 23 to July 24, 1984; and April 23 to August 2, 1986. It is most numerous in the lower canyons during the first half of May, when hundreds of spring migrants are moving through. Clyde and Lois Harden and I banded more than two dozen at Springdale and in Oak Creek Canyon from April 24 to June 15, 1963. Post-nesting birds generally remain on their breeding grounds until late August, before departing for their wintering grounds to the south. There are only a few scattered September reports; the latest is two individuals at the Zion Lodge on September 23, 1971 (Gifford).

Blue Grosbeak. *Guiraca caerulea.*
Fairly common summer resident.

This attractive bird resides only in the lowlands, along the Virgin River and in side-canyons. Records extend from April 26 to October 26, although the majority of reports occur between early May and mid-September. Jerome Gifford recorded arrival and departure dates at Springdale during six seasons: from May 18 to September 25, 1974; April 29 to October 18, 1975; April 26 to September 17, 1979; May 3 to September 12, 1982; May 4 to July 21, 1985; and May 9 to August 31, 1986.

Nesting has been recorded on numerous occasions: I found adults feeding young birds at the Springdale Ponds on July 6, 1965; F. Winch reported a nest "located in a small maple at eye-level" (NPS files) along the Riverside Walk on May 10, 1968. Jerome Gifford recorded territorial pairs on three breeding bird census plots: one pair in Coalpits Wash from June 3 to July 8, 1979; three pairs at Grafton from May 13 to July 15, 1979; and one pair at Springdale from May 18 to August 15, 1978. Adult males usually leave their nesting grounds by mid-August, but females and juveniles may remain into October. The latest report is one at Springdale on October 18, 1975 (Gifford).

Lazuli Bunting. *Passerina amoena.*
Common summer resident and migrant.

This is one of the area's most attractive songbirds. It has been reported as early as April 12 (Shane Pruett reported one singing in Oak Creek Canyon in 1993) and as late as October 14. Summer residents are restricted to lowland nesting sites along the brushy floodplain and side-canyons up to about 5,000 feet. Jerome Gifford recorded territorial pairs on three breeding bird census plots: at Springdale from May 29 to July 26, 1978; in the Watchman Campground from May 13 to July 27, 1980; and in Heaps' Canyon from May 15 to July 17, 1983.

Post-nesting birds often congregate in flocks and feed along the weedy roadsides. Gifford reported a high of 30 birds at Springdale on August 30, 1983. And migrants can appear almost anywhere; I banded two birds in Potato Hollow on August 6 and 7, 1965. There are only scattered reports after mid-September, and the latest fall record is a lone female at Grafton on October 13 and 14, 1981 (Gifford).

Indigo Bunting. *Passerina cyanea.*
Rare summer resident and migrant.

Records extend from April 30 to September 7, although the majority of reports occur from late May to early August. During three seasons,

Lazuli Bunting

Jerome Gifford recorded birds at Springdale consistently from May 30 to September 2, 1976; from June 21 to July 25, 1977; and from May 28 to June 26, 1978. It also nests some years, utilizing brushy vegetation along the Virgin River and in adjacent side-canyons. Gifford found a nest in a tangle of wild roses at Springdale in June 1964, and he recorded territorial pairs on two breeding bird census plots: one pair at Springdale from May 30 to August 15, 1976, and one pair in Heaps' Canyon from May 1 to June 11, 1982. Post-nesting birds wander throughout the lowlands, and the majority leave the area by early August.

SUBFAMILY EMBERIZINAE: EMBERIZINES:
TOWHEES AND SPARROWS

Green-tailed Towhee. *Pipilo chlorurus.*
Common summer resident and migrant.
This lovely bird nests in brushy areas in the ponderosa pine zone and into the higher pine-fir-aspen community. I found a nest, containing

Green-tailed Towhee

four eggs, on a white fir at Blue Springs Lake on June 9, 1965. Jerome Gifford recorded territorial pairs on two 40-acre breeding bird census plots: two pairs were near the East Entrance from May 14 to July 15, 1978, and again from May 22 to July 22, 1979; and four pairs were at Lava Point from June 4 to July 24, 1978.

Spring migrants may appear as early as April 3 (I found one in Coalpits Wash in 1963), but they are more numerous by mid-April; I banded more than two dozen in Oak Creek Canyon from April 16 to May 20, 1963. Post-nesting birds can be found almost anywhere in the high country. Clyde and Lois Harden banded birds at the Lamoreaux Ranch on July 17, 18, 26 and 27, and August 5, 1965; and a few were still present in this area on October 2, 1995 (Wauer). Fall migrants may appear in the lowlands by late August, but are never as numerous as they are in spring. They occasionally linger through December; it was reported on only two of 25 CBCs (1970–94): two individuals were seen in both 1974 and 1987.

Spotted Towhee. *Pipilo maculatus.*
Common summer and winter resident.

This bird was known as the Rufous-sided Towhee until 1996, which was split into two species by the AOU (1996): the Spotted Towhee of the West and the Eastern Towhee of eastern North America. At ZNP, some birds undoubtedly are permanent residents, but there are significant seasonal population fluctuations. Nesting occurs at brushy area at all elevations. Jerome Gifford recorded territorial pairs on six breeding bird census plots: in Parunuweap Canyon from May 31 to July 18, 1981, and again from May 14 to July 16, 1982; at Springdale from June 13 to 27, 1976; near the Temple of Sinawava from June 10 to July 14, 1983; a high of 11 pairs was recorded on a 50-acre plot in Heaps' Canyon from May 24 to July 17, 1982; at the East Entrance from June 5 to July 31, 1977, and again from May 14 to July 15, 1978; and at Lava Point on June 4 to July 24, 1978.

Post-nesting birds in the high country usually remain on their territories until the first cold fronts arrive in fall or early winter. They may then move to lower, warmer areas. In late winter and early spring, birds may move up and down the slopes in concert with each warm and cold spell. I discovered 80 individuals near the ZCVC during a snowstorm on March 25, 1964. It was recorded on all 25 (1970–94) CBCs, with an average of 15 individuals and a high count of 78 on December 17, 1973.

Abert's Towhee. *Pipilo aberti.*
Casual late fall and winter visitor.

Records extend from September 26 to January 6, all from the Virgin River between Parunuweap Canyon and Springdale. This towhee nests on the Virgin River floodplain in the Santa Clara and St. George area and southward; and post-nesting birds wander up-river, occasionally reaching the Zion Park area by fall. The earliest report is one found in Parunuweap Canyon on September 26, 1995 (Wauer), and the latest record is one at Springdale on January 5 and 6, 1979 (Jerome Gifford).

Rufous-crowned Sparrow. *Aimophila ruficeps.*
Rare permanent resident.

The first record for ZNP and Utah was one captured in a mist net in Oak Creek Canyon on November 3, 1963, and at least six individuals were present in the area all winter of 1963–64 (Wauer 1965). Dennis Carter also observed two birds in Pine Creek Canyon on November 6, and he found a dead bird there on November 12. Five additional Rufous-crowned Sparrows were banded in Oak Creek Canyon during August and October 1964, and one of the banded birds was seen there throughout December; another was banded there on January 30, 1965. And on August 10, 1965, I collected an immature bird in Oak Creek Canyon, indicating that it also nests on the upper slopes of the lower canyons and moves to the lowlands after nesting and to winter.

To test this theory, I searched appropriate habitats during May and June, 1966; on June 29, I discovered a singing adult on the west slope of Steven's Wash in Parunuweap Canyon. While watching this bird, a second Rufous-crowned Sparrow appeared nearby, its bill full of nesting material. Both birds then flew up the slope and out of sight (Wauer 1967).

Since those first reports, it has been recorded on several other occasions and at various localities. Jerome Gifford recorded a territorial pair on a breeding bird census plot in Parunuweap Canyon from May 25 to July 7, 1980; and in 1985, he recorded it there almost daily all year. It was also recorded on 14 of 25 CBCs (1970–94), including a high count of 11 on December 18, 1976. More recently, Mark Bromley found it on the hillside near Virgin on June 1, 1982. It undoubtedly is a year-round resident in the Zion Park area.

American Tree Sparrow. *Spizella arborea.*
Two records.

One collected in Oak Creek Canyon on November 19, 1965, represents the first record for the Zion Park area (Wauer 1969). A second bird was reported for Springdale on March 29, 1973 (Jerome Gifford). Although this sparrow is extremely rare in southern Utah in winter, it is "a rather common winter resident in the central valleys of the state from late September to early May" (Hayward et al. 1976).

Chipping Sparrow. *Spizella passerina.*
Common summer resident; abundant migrant; casual in winter.

This little, reddish-capped bird is the park's most common sparrow in spring and summer. Early spring migrants appear during the second week of April, and it can be abundant from the end of the month to mid-May. Jerome Gifford found 100 to 200 individuals at Springdale during all of May and June 1975. I found nesting birds in Cave Valley on June 1, 1965, and Gifford recorded three territorial pairs on a 40-acre breeding bird census plot at the East Entrance from May 14 to July 15, 1978; he also found five pairs there from May 22 to July 22, 1979.

Post-nesting birds wander throughout the high country, often forming huge flocks. Clyde and Lois Harden banded more than a dozen at the Lamoreaux Ranch from July 17 to August 9, 1964; and Betty and I encountered a flock of 200-plus along the North Fork Road on September 27, 1995. Fall migrants usually occur in the lowlands from early September through October, but they are never as numerous as they are in spring. There also are scattered winter reports at Springdale from December 9 to January 19; it was recorded on five of 25 CBCs (1970–94), including a high count of 12 on December 18, 1976.

Brewer's Sparrow. *Spizella breweri.*
Uncommon summer resident; fairly common migrant; casual in winter.

This little sparrow is a summer resident on sagebrush flats in the high country, although nesting has not been documented. The earliest spring migrant was one found at Springdale on March 30, 1983 (Jerome Gifford). It is most numerous from April 11 through May; I found flocks of five and eight birds in Coalpits Wash on April 11, 1963, and a high of 60 in Coalpits Wash on May 6, 1965. Fall migrants may appear in the lowlands during the second week of August, and there are scattered reports to October 22. There are no November records, but Gifford recorded two in Hepworth Wash on December 16 and 18, 1982, and four and two at Springdale on December 27, 1969, and December 29, 1971, respectively. It was recorded on five of 25 CBCs (1970–94), including a high of 12 birds on December 18, 1976. There are no reports for January and February.

Black-chinned Sparrow. *Spizella atrogularis.*
Rare summer resident and migrant.

Records extend from April 11 to October 28, but only the summer resident birds can be found with any certainty. Breeding birds utilize brushy areas in side-canyons at mid-elevations and in the high country. I banded an immature bird in Oak Creek Canyon on July 3, 1963, found several juveniles in Cave Valley on July 29, 1963, and recorded five singing territorial birds (all from one spot) on Firepit Knoll, June 1, 1965. There are additional June and July reports from Taylor Creek, Hepworth Wash, and Scoggin's Wash. Post-nesting birds apparently remain on their breeding grounds until mid-September; Steve Summers reported 12 individuals (all were immatures but one) in Kolob Canyon on August 6, 1994, and there are scattered fall reports from Hepworth Wash, Cave Valley, and the North Fork Road. There also are two October reports: Jerome Gifford found lone birds in Coalpits Wash on October 3 and 28, 1972.

Vesper Sparrow. *Pooecetes gramineus.*
Fairly common summer resident and migrant.

It arrives in mid-March and may be numerous in the lower canyons from the end of the month to the first of May; a few usually linger until late May. Vesper Sparrows frequent grassy areas in the lower canyons, especially during stormy weather; 20 were seen at the ZCVC on May 5, 1964. Nesting birds utilize sagebrush flats in the high country; I found a nesting pair at Blue Springs Lake on June 11, 1965, and Jerome Gifford recorded four territorial pairs on a 40-acre breeding bird census plot at Lava Point from June 4 to July 24, 1978.

Post-nesting birds and fall migrants congregate in open fields and pastures at least until late September. Clyde and Lois Harden banded several at the Lamoreaux Ranch on July 22 and 27, 1965; I banded one at Blue Springs Lake on August 31, 1965; and Gifford recorded 30 and 40 individuals on the Kolob Terrace on September 18, 1974, and September 14, 1975, respectively. The latest fall record is one in Cave Valley on October 2, 1995 (Wauer). And it was recorded on only two of 25 CBCs (1970–94): two on December 17, 1973, and two on December 28, 1987.

Lark Sparrow. *Chondestes grammacus.*
Uncommon summer resident and migrant; casual in winter.

This well-marked sparrow frequents grassy and sagebrush flats below the ponderosa pine forest at mid-elevations and fields in the Virgin River Valley. There are several reports of nesting: I found singing birds in Cave Valley and also on Firepit Knoll on June 1,

Lark Sparrow

1965, and young birds at Firepit Knoll on June 9. And Jerome Gifford reported nesting pairs in the Watchman Campground on May 6, 1983, and at Grafton on July 12, 1981.

It is most numerous during the spring migration, beginning in mid-April and peaking during the first three weeks of May. Gifford reported high counts of 20 and 40 individuals at Springdale on May 6 and 7, 1975, and 30 at both Springdale and Grafton on May 4 and 9, 1984, respectively. Post-nesting birds and fall migrants can appear almost anywhere; I banded one at Potato Hollow on August 8, 1965. It is fairly common in the lowlands to late September, after which there are only a few reports to late October. There are no records in November, but there are several during the winter months: I found three below Rockville on December 29, 1964; Louise Excell recorded two in Springdale on January 14 and February 26, 1984; and Gifford recorded it at Grafton on February 17, 1983, and March 18, 1984.

Black-throated Sparrow. *Amphispiza bilineata.*
Common summer resident and casual winter visitor.

This is the desert sparrow that resides only in the desert lowlands, especially in blackbrush communities. Jerome Gifford recorded 28 territorial pairs on a 160-acre breeding bird census plot in Coalpits Wash from April 15 to July 2, 1979, and he also found a nest, with three nestlings, at Springdale on June 21, 1986. Immediately after nesting, it wanders to higher, somewhat cooler elevations for the summer. Andrew Core found it on the Watchman Trail on June 5, 1995. And it usually leaves the area entirely by the end of August, although a few may remain in the lowlands during warm winters. There are scattered reports at Coalpits Wash, Rockville, and Springdale, and it was recorded on one (December 27, 1989) of 25 CBCs (1970–94).

Sage Sparrow. *Amphispiza belli.*
Rare migrant and winter resident.

Records of this Great Basin species occur in the Zion Park area almost every month, but it is most often reported during the winter months from late November to mid-March. It was recorded on only four of 25 CBCs (1970–94), with a high count of nine on December 28, 1981. Although the majority of the winter reports are from the lowlands at Coalpits Wash, Grafton, and Rockville, it also has been found in winter at the East Entrance and Hop Valley. I found several birds at the ZCVC during a snowstorm on March 16, 1963. And there are several unexpected sightings at Grafton: Jerome Gifford found one there on May 13, 1979; three on May 16, 1983, and 12, 10, and three individuals there on July 28, 29, and 30, 1981, respectively; and one on October 18, 1983. The July reports suggest that it may nest in the surrounding area.

Savannah Sparrow. *Passerculus sandwichensis.*
Fairly common spring migrant; rare fall migrant; uncommon winter visitor.

It has been recorded in the Zion Park area every month but June and July. The earliest fall reports include birds banded at the Lamoreaux Ranch on August 9 and September 4, 1965 (Clyde and Lois Harden). There are scattered lowland reports in September and October, and increased reports from early December, through the winter months, to two late spring reports at Springdale on May 8, 1979 and 1981 (Jerome Gifford). A high number of 16 birds was reported at Grafton on March 22, 1985 (Gifford). And CBC participants recorded it in only three of 25 years (1970–94). It is most numerous as a spring migrant in the lowlands from early March to mid-April, and there is a second movement during late April and early May.

Fox Sparrow. *Passerella iliaca.*
Casual migrant and winter visitor.

The first report was by Clifford Presnall, who claimed that it was an "uncommon winter visitant in the canyon from September to late March" (Presnall 1935). Later records, although few and far between, support Presnall's time frame. The earliest fall report is one at Springdale on September 20 and 21, 1981 (Jerome Gifford); I banded one in Oak Creek Canyon on October 27, 1963, and observed one at Springdale on November 20, 1965. It has been reported on seven occasions in December, including one or two birds on three of 25 CBCs (1970–94); and S. Schneider reported one on January 1, 1991, that had been "seen several times over the previous two weeks" (NPS files) at a bird feeder at the Kolob Canyon Visitor Center. And finally, there are three spring reports: Steve Hedges observed two at the Springdale Ponds on March 6, 1976; and I recorded lone birds at Springdale on March 25, 1963, and in Oak Creek Canyon on April 27, 1965.

Song Sparrow. *Melospiza melodia.*
Fairly common summer resident; common migrant and winter resident.

This little sparrow is almost always associated with wetlands. Jerome Gifford recorded territorial pairs on three breeding bird census plots: one pair on a 60-acre plot at Grafton from May 13 to July 15, 1979; three pairs on a 26-acre plot at Springdale from April 23 to July 10, 1978; and one or two pairs at Watercress Spring along the Riverside Walk from May 26 to July 14, 1983 and again in 1986.

It is most numerous during migration from late March to early June in spring, and from early September through October in fall. Although the majority of these reports are from the lowlands, it occasionally can also be found in the high country. Winter residents are reasonably stable by early December, and CBC participants recorded it all 25 years (1970–94); 10 or fewer birds were tallied

Song Sparrow

seven years, and 30 or more birds were tallied five years, including a high count of 49 on December 17, 1973.

Lincoln's Sparrow. *Melospiza lincolnii.*
Rare summer and uncommon winter resident; fairly common migrant.

This perky little sparrow has been recorded every month but August. There are two nesting records, both in the high country at wetland sites: Clyde and Lois Harden found a nest, containing four young, below the Kolob Reservoir on June 27, 1965; and Jerome Gifford found one on a 40-acre breeding bird census plot at Lava Point from May 11 to 19, 1978. Post-nesting birds remain in the high country at wet areas and in weedy fields all summer; Hardens banded three at the Lamoreaux Ranch on July 17, 18, and 24, 1965.

Early fall migrants may appear in the lowlands in early September (Gifford found five at Springdale on September 6, 1979), but they normally do not arrive until the end of the month or later. During four winter seasons, Gifford recorded arrival and departure dates at Springdale from October 24, 1980, to May 29, 1981; September 29, 1981, to April 19, 1982; October 6, 1982, to May 2, 1983; and October 5, 1983, to May 10, 1984. Winter birds frequent weedy areas along the Virgin River and in side-canyons, and often associate with the more common White-crowned Sparrows. It was recorded on 15 of 25 CBCs (1970–94), with a high count of seven birds on December 28, 1978. Spring migrants appear in the canyons by the end of February, increase during March and April, and a few can still be found until mid-May. I banded more than three dozen individuals at Springdale and Oak Creek Canyon between February 25 and May 11, 1963.

Swamp Sparrow. *Melospiza georgiana.*
One record.

One collected at the Springdale Ponds on March 2, 1965, represents the first for ZNP and only the second for southern Utah (Wauer and Russell 1967). This wetland sparrow is an extremely rare winter visitor in southern Utah, although it is more numerous in the northern portion of the state (Behle et al. 1985).

White-throated Sparrow. *Zonotrichia albicollis.*
Rare winter resident.

Records extend from September 29 (Jerome Gifford found one at Springdale in 1987), through the winter months, to May 6; one was found at Springdale in 1973 (Gifford). Gifford recorded it at Springdale almost daily during two winter seasons: from December 12, 1983, to May 1, 1984, and October 23 to April 24, 1985. And it was recorded on four of 25 CBCs (1970–94), with lone birds in December 1979, 1980, 1983, and 1984, and a high of three individuals on December 27, 1994. All reports are from the vicinity of the Virgin River, except for one female (of at least two individuals heard singing in Oak Creek Canyon) collected on October 29, 1965 (Wauer and Russell 1967).

Golden-crowned Sparrow. *Zonotrichia atricapilla.*
Casual migrant and rare winter resident.

Records of this West Coast sparrow extend from October 8, through the winter months, to May 22, all from the lowlands, and include five

White-crowned Sparrow

banded birds in Oak Creek Canyon on October 29 and November 4, 14, 16, and 18, 1965 (Wauer and Russell 1967). It is most numerous from early November to early January, there are scattered reports to mid-April, and there is a brief surge in late April. In 1982–83, Jerome Gifford recorded it almost daily at Springdale from December 4 to May 23, and lone birds were recorded on three of 25 CBCs (1970–94), in December 1982, 1986, and 1988.

White-crowned Sparrow. *Zonotrichia leucophrys.*
Abundant migrant and winter resident.

This is one of the area's most numerous winter residents in the lowlands; an average of 327 individuals were recorded on 25 CBCs (1970–94), with 200 or more individuals tallied 17 years, and high counts of 1,051 and 905 on December 17, 1973, and December 27, 1989, respectively. Overall, records extend from August 14, through the winter months, to June 9; these early and late reports include one on the Kolob Reservoir Road on August 14, 1975 (Jerome Gifford), and one at Blue Springs Lake on June 9, 1965 (Wauer). During six seasons, Gifford recorded arrival and departure dates at Springdale from October 8, 1973, to April 28, 1974; September 2, 1974, to May 21, 1975; October 1, 1975, to May 7, 1976; September 30, 1979, to May 27, 1980; September 13, 1980, to May 18, 1981; and September 27, 1983, to May 8, 1984.

The earliest fall migrants represent the race *oriantha*, which nests in Utah, but the later more numerous winter birds represent the race *gambeli*, which nests in the Northwest—from British Columbia to northern Saskatchewan, Canada, and north to north-central Alaska (AOU 1957). From fall 1963 to mid-summer 1965, I banded a total of 533 White-crowned Sparrows, primarily at Springdale, Watchman orchards, and Oak Creek Canyon. Of all those birds, only one was reported elsewhere: one banded at Springdale on January 31, 1965, was retaken at Brookings, Oregon, on April 21, 1965.

Dark-eyed Junco. *Junco hyemalis.*
Fairly common summer resident; abundant migrant and winter resident.

Until 1983, this bird was divided into three distinctly marked species: Slate-colored, Oregon, and Gray-headed juncos. Since all three of these forms occur in the Zion Park area, and records were maintained separately until they were lumped together by the AOU, the three juncos will be discussed separately. However, all three over-winter together in the lower canyons, and move up and down the slopes in response to local weather conditions. On warm, sunny days, the majority of the populations are likely to move onto the higher slopes, but cold fronts, especially those with blowing snow, will trigger an immediate return to the more protected lowlands. This altitudinal ebb-and-flow continues all winter, at least until late April, when the increasing daylight and spring-like conditions to the north entice them toward their breeding grounds.

Slate-colored Juncos are uncommon winter residents only. Arrival and departure dates at Springdale were recorded on four seasons by Jerome Gifford: from December 12, 1974, to March 28, 1975; November 18, 1976, to March 31, 1977; November 6, 1979, to April 5, 1980; and October 20, 1984, to March 11, 1985. The latest report was a lone bird at the South Campground on April 14, 1980 (Gifford). Also, it was recorded on 10 of 25 CBCs (1970–94); one to nine individuals were tallied on eight counts, and a high of 52 individuals were recorded on December 30, 1980.

Oregon Juncos are common migrants and abundant winter residents. This bird is the single most numerous winter bird below the higher terraces, although somewhat sporadic in the lower canyons. Jerome Gifford recorded arrival and departure dates at Springdale during seven seasons: from October 21, 1973, to March 14, 1974; October 23, 1974, to May 18, 1975; October 30, 1977, to May 5, 1978; October 19, 1980, to April 7, 1981; October 10, 1982, to April 26, 1983; October 3, 1984, to April 11, 1985; and September 24, 1986, to March 6, 1987. Gifford's highest count was 300 individuals at Springdale on January 1, 1974. And CBC participants recorded it on 15 of 25 years (1970–94), with more than 500 individuals tallied seven times; a high count of 871 was recorded on December 19, 1972. An even higher count of 1,113 individuals was tallied on the December 1964 CBC (Wauer 1965c).

From late summer 1963 to mid-summer 1966, I banded a total of 1,905 individuals, primarily at Oak Creek Canyon. During that period, I captured only one bird that had been banded elsewhere: an adult male on February 27, 1966, that had been banded at Salt Lake City, Utah, on February 16, 1964.

Gray-headed Juncos are the full-time resident juncos in the Zion Park area, although they, too, are subject to altitudinal movements with the seasons. Breeding birds reside in the pine-fir-aspen habitats in the high country: Cindy Beaudett and Judy Vavra reported "adults with two fledglings" (NPS files) in Hidden Canyon on June 22, 1982, and Jerome Gifford recorded four territorial pairs on a 40-acre breeding bird census plot at Lava Point from June 4 to July 24, 1978. Post-nesting birds remain in the high country at least until mid-October. Clyde and Lois Harden banded birds at the Lamoreaux Ranch on July 17 and August 8, 1965, and I banded several at Potato Hollow on August 9, 1965.

The earliest lowland report in fall is by Jerome Gifford who found two birds at Springdale on October 16, 1987. He also recorded arrival and departure dates at Springdale on four seasons: from November 25, 1983, to April 25, 1984; November 28, 1975, to April 18, 1976; October 19, 1981, to April 3, 1982; and October 20, 1984, to April 27, 1985. Christmas Bird Count participants reported it on 19 of 25 years (1970–94), with an average of 79 birds and a high count of 857 on December 28, 1992.

From late 1963 to mid-summer 1966, I banded a total of 1,159 Gray-headed Juncos, with the vast majority of those captured in Oak Creek Canyon. The largest numbers were recorded during periods of stormy weather: several hundred individuals were present around the ZCVC during a heavy snowstorm on March 16 and 17, 1963, and also during heavy rains on April 17, 1963 (Wauer). After mid-May, it lingers only at feeders, but even these move on to their breeding grounds by the end of the month.

SUBFAMILY ICTERINAE: ICTERINES:
BLACKBIRDS, MEADOWLARKS, AND COWBIRDS

Red-winged Blackbird. *Agelaius phoeniceus.*
Fairly common summer resident; sporadic winter resident; fairly common migrant.

This well-known blackbird is a full-time resident at the Grafton Ponds, but irregular elsewhere. It was found nesting in a cattail wetland in Parunuweap Canyon on May 4, 1965, and at the Springdale Ponds on May 25, 1965 (Wauer); and Jerome Gifford recorded 14 territorial pairs on a 26-acre breeding bird census plot at Springdale from April 23 to July 10, 1978. Post-nesting birds may move to cooler locations during the hottest summer days. These birds, and perhaps others, return in August, September, or October. Gifford recorded arrival and departure dates at Springdale and Grafton during five winter seasons: the Springdale reports are from September 4, 1974, to July 17, 1975; October 1, 1975, to August 8, 1976; September 28, 1977, to July 30, 1978; and October 8, 1981, to July 6, 1982; and the Grafton reports are from August 13, 1985, to September 9, 1986 (year-round).

Winter populations can be rather extensive; Gifford reported 4,000 at Springdale on November 21, 1977, although counts of 400 to 800 were more typical. Christmas Bird Count participants missed it only three times in 25 years (1970–94), tallying an average of 40 individuals and a high count of 352 on December 31, 1975.

Western Meadowlark

Western Meadowlark. *Sturnella neglecta.*
Uncommon summer resident and sporadic winter visitor.

It is present year-round in fields and pastures in the lower Virgin River Valley, although it may move about in response to weather conditions and food. Russell Grater (1947) first mentioned that it nested in the "lower portions of the park" in May and June, and Jerome Gifford recorded two territorial pairs on a 60-acre breeding bird census plot at Grafton from May 13 to July 15, 1979. Post-nesting birds may move up-canyon; Gordon Gover found up to seven birds in the Watchman area on June 1, 1994, and Gifford found 14 at a mulberry tree in the middle of Springdale on June 28, 1979.

The resident birds, and possibly other populations from more northerly breeding grounds, normally return to the lower valley by late October and remain through the winter months. Christmas Bird Count participants recorded it on 19 of 25 years (1970–94), with an average of 13 birds, and a high count of 62 on December 27, 1988.

Yellow-headed Blackbird. *Xanthocephalus xanthocephalus.*
Uncommon migrant.

The majority of reports are of one to a few Yellow-heads in small mixed flocks with Brewer's Blackbirds and Brown-headed Cowbirds. Spring records extend from March 30 to June 24, all from the lowlands, except for three birds with a flock of Brewer's Blackbirds near the Kolob Reservoir on May 27, 1965 (Wauer). Jerome Gifford recorded a spring high of 10 individuals at Springdale on May 20, 1981. Post-nesting birds and fall migrants may appear in the lowlands as early as July 9 and remain as late as October 6. Two males were recorded at the Grafton Ponds in 1986 (Gifford). Gifford reported a high fall count of 29 near Virgin on September 11, 1981. And there is a single winter report: Vince Mowbray and Louise Excell found a flock of 10 individuals at "Zion" on January 19, 1980 (Kingery 1980).

Brewer's Blackbird. *Euphagus cyanocephalus.*
Uncommon summer resident; fairly common migrant; sporadic winter visitor.

This all-dark blackbird nests only in the high country; I found five territorial pairs near the Kolob Reservoir on June 1, 1965, and three nests at Blue Springs Lake: one singing male and a nest containing five eggs two feet high in a willow on June 1, 1965, as well as one nest in a willow and another on the ground under a big sagebrush on June 9, 1965. Post-nesting birds wander considerably, sometimes forming huge flocks: I found a small flock at Lava Point on June 27, 1963, and Jerome Gifford reported a flock of 300 birds at the Kolob Reservoir on September 18, 1974. Flocks may remain at the Kolob Reservoir and Blue Springs Lake until the first of October.

Fall migrants may appear in the lowlands by the first week of September, increase during late September and early October, and there are scattered reports throughout the remainder of the fall and winter months. Gifford reported a high fall count of 400 birds at Grafton on November 25, 1983. It was recorded on only five of 25 CBCs (1970–94), with totals of two and six birds in December 1973 and 1981, and 32, 38, and 35 in December 1976, 1977, and 1979, respectively. And the first of the spring migrants normally appear in the lowlands the first week of April, peak during mid-April, and a few may linger at certain localities (such as the Grafton Ponds) until early July.

Great-tailed Grackle. *Quiscalus mexicanus.*
Casual visitor.

This southern blackbird moved into southwestern Utah during the 1980s, and it has been reported in the Zion Park area only since 1984; it is likely to increase along the Virgin River Valley. The first Utah nest was reported at Ivins Reservoir on May 20, 1983 (Steve Hedges). Dane Gifford was first to record this bird (three males) at Springdale on May 16, 1984; they were also observed by Jewel and Jerome Gifford, Louise Excell, and Kirk Topham, and were photographed by Jerome. Two individuals were next reported at Rockville on April 9 and 12, 1985 (Vickie Parkinson), and Jerome Gifford found a lone male at the Grafton Ponds on April 14, 1985.

Brown-headed Cowbird. *Molothrus ater.*
Common summer resident and spring migrant.

Records extend from March 25 to August 5, and there are three later reports: Jerome Gifford found lone birds at Springdale on August 26 and September 6, 1976, and I recorded three at Blue Springs Lake on August 30, 1965. And there also is a lone winter report; I found a lone bird in Cave Valley on February 22, 1964.

Gifford recorded arrival and departure dates at Springdale during seven seasons: from April 18 to July 11, 1974; April 24 to August 5, 1976; May 5 to July 21, 1978; April 18 to July 28, 1979; May 13 to July 14, 1981; May 14 to July 28, 1983; and March 25 to July 26, 1984. High counts include 50 in a field at Springdale on May 13, 1965 (Wauer), and 50 at Springdale on May 1, 1975, and April 28, 1984 (Gifford).

Gifford recorded breeding birds on three breeding bird census plots: five pairs on a 60-acre plot at Grafton from May 13 to July 15, 1979; one pair on a 26-acre plot at Springdale from April 23 to July 10, 1978; and one pair on a 40-acre plot at the confluence of Pine and Clear Creeks from May 25 to July 20, 1980. He also found Cowbird eggs in four House Sparrow nests at the Driftwood Lodge in Springdale during spring 1979.

Hooded Oriole. *Icterus cucullatus.*
Casual spring/summer visitor.

Records extend from April 13 to August 9. Although there are no nesting reports, it should be expected; breeding birds have been recorded at Littlefield and in Beaver Dam Wash, Washington County, Utah (Wauer 1969; Hayward et al. 1976). The first Zion Park area report was a male found at a Springdale bird feeder by Richard Fesler on April 13, 1976; it remained four days and was seen by several others, including Jerome Gifford. A female or immature male was next reported for the Watchman Campground by Josh Brack on May 7, 1981; Gifford found one at his Springdale feeders on July 23 and 24, 1981, and again from August 6 to 9, 1982; Hugh and Marsha Bain reported one at upper Emerald Pools Canyon on June 28, 1983; Myrtle and Denver Smith observed a female in the Watchman Residential Area on May 17, 1985; and Kevin Wallace reported a male at Mooney's Pond in Rockville on May 9, 1987.

Bullock's Oriole. *Icterus bullockii.*
Common summer resident.

The name of this species has recently been reallocated back to the name Bullock's from Northern Oriole (AOU 1996). Records extend from April 10 to September 30. Jerome Gifford recorded arrival and departure dates at Springdale during 12 consecutive seasons: from April 24 to July 31, 1976; April 20 to July 28, 1977; April 20 to September 6, 1978; April 16 to August 25, 1979; April 27 to August 21, 1980; April 16 to August 11, 1981; April 18 to August 23, 1982; April 19 to August 25, 1983; April 10 to July 31, 1984; April 13 to July 21, 1985; April 22 to August 7, 1986; and April 10 to August 13, 1987.

Nest-building normally begins soon after it arrives, and Gifford recorded territorial pairs on three breeding bird census plots: two pairs on a 160-acre plot in Coalpits Wash from April 15 to July 2, 1979; six pairs on a 60-acre plot at Grafton from May 13 to July 15, 1978; and two pairs on a 26-acre plot at Springdale from April 23 to July 10, 1978. Post-nesting birds often join other family groups, and flocks may consist of four or five families; Gifford reported a flock of 21 individuals at Springdale on June 7, 1984. They usually remain in the area at least to late July, and there are scattered reports to September 30; I observed a female or immature bird in Springdale on September 6, 1995.

Scott's Oriole. *Icterus parisorum.*
Casual summer resident.

It has been reported in the Zion Park area, in both the riparian and pinyon-juniper woodlands, as early as April 27 (one at the South Campground in 1993 by Jim and Shirley Thielen) until as late as July 28; one or more fed at hummingbird feeders in Springdale all during July 1984 and 1986 (Jerome Gifford). And from May 5 to 8, 1976, one was in the company of a Hooded Oriole (Gifford). However, there is no sure evidence of nesting, although Eric Haskell found a singing male in Hepworth Wash on May 8, 1994.

SUBFAMILY CARDUELINAE: CARDUELINE FINCHES

Gray-crowned Rosy-Finch. *Leucosticte tephrocotis.*
Casual winter visitor.

Clifford Presnall was first to report this boreal finch; he found a flock of 75 on Birch Creek on January 21, 1935, and a large flock at the East Entrance on March 15, 1935 (Presnall 1935). He wrote that they "winter in the higher and more rugged portions of the park, and irregularly in the canyons. Sight records indicate that these are mixed flocks apparently composed of this form and Hepburns [Black-capped] Rosy Finch, with a few Black Rosy Finches." W. S. Long next reported a large flock near the East Entrance on February 3, 1936; Richard A. Stuart found a flock of about 50 birds five miles east of the East Entrance on January 31, 1973; Jerome Gifford recorded 30 at Clear Creek on December 18, 1982; and Robert Rucker reported one near Observation Point on November 12, 1994.

Cassin's Finch. *Carpodacus cassinii.*
Fairly common summer resident and a sporadic winter visitor.

This is the finch of the pinyon-juniper woodlands and high country forests and adjacent clearings. I found a nest on a white fir at Blue Springs Lake on June 6, 1965. Jerome Gifford recorded territorial pairs on three 40-acre breeding bird census plots: 1.5 pairs at the confluence of Pine and Clear Creeks from May 25 to July 20, 1980; six pairs at the East Entrance from May 14 to July 15, 1978, and four pairs there from May 22 to July 22, 1979; and three pairs at Lava Point from June 4 to July 24, 1978.

Post-nesting birds spend the summer and fall months at old fields and clearings in the high country. Clyde and Lois Harden banded birds at the Lamoreaux Ranch on July 18 and August 3 and 8, 1965; I found it common at Blue Springs Lake on August 30, 1964, and also along the Kolob Terrace Road above Cave Valley on October 2, 1995. A few individuals move into the lowlands as early as the second week of September, and there are scattered reports in the lowlands and elsewhere (i.e. East Entrance) all winter. However, it was recorded on CBCs only seven times in 25 years (1970–94), including one to four birds in five years and 13 and 14 individuals on December 28, 1981, and December 27, 1989, respectively. Gifford reported a high count of 80 individuals at Grafton on February 5, 1982. Winter birds sometimes linger in the lowlands until early May.

House Finch. *Carpodacus mexicanus.*
Abundant permanent resident.

No other bird represents the arid lowlands so well as this active little songster. House Finches are one of the few birds that sing on sunny days in winter, and breeding birds frequent desert washes and slopes up into the pinyon-juniper woodlands. I found a nest, containing three eggs, on a cholla cactus in Coalpits Wash on April 11, 1963, and fledglings at Springdale on May 25, 1965. Jerome Gifford recorded territorial pairs on three breeding bird census plots: 3.5 pairs on a 160-acre plot in Coalpits Wash from April 15 to July 2, 1979; 12 pairs on a 60-acre plot at Grafton from May 13 to July 15, 1979; and three pairs on a 26-acre plot at Springdale from April 23 to July 10, 1978.

Post-nesting birds practically desert their lowland nesting sites, moving into cooler canyons and onto the higher terraces. But they return to the lowlands, often in huge flocks, by early to late September. They may remain in these flocks all winter. An average of 178 House Finches were tallied on 25 CBCs (1970–94): more than 200 individuals were found on 10 different years, with high counts of 380 individuals on December 28, 1992, and December 27, 1993.

Red Crossbill. *Loxia curvirostra.*
Sporadic visitor.

This high country finch can appear almost any time of the year, although the majority of the reports occur from late summer to early winter. The first two Zion Park reports included a specimen taken on the East Rim "in the summer of 1931," and "a small flock in November, 1934" in Potato Hollow (Presnall 1935). It was not reported again until 1963, when Dennis Carter and I found eight birds northwest of Lava Point on October 21; then I recorded eight on Maloney Hill on October 31, and 20 individuals on the east side of the park on November 7. I also found a lone bird on Deertrap Mountain on May 11, 1964.

It was next recorded in the spring of 1981, when Robert Tweit reported "great numbers of adult and immature Red Crossbills on Horse Pasture Plateau," between Lava Point and Potato Hollow. Tweit told Jerome Gifford that he was "certain that they had nested in the area" (Gifford 1987). There are two additional reports: Gifford found 11 on Cable Mountain on December 19, 1983, and R. Woodward reported a pair feeding on ponderosa pine cones on Northgate Peak on May 13, 1995.

Pine Siskin. *Carduelis pinus.*
Fairly common migrant and winter visitor.

Like most of the Cardueline finches, this tiny bird wanders irregularly, resulting in sporadic occurrences. Although it has been reported in the Zion Park area year-round, it is most numerous in the lowlands in winter. During seven seasons, Jerome Gifford recorded arrival and departure dates at Springdale from October 10, 1974, to May 17, 1975; November 2, 1975, to April 22, 1976; October 21, 1978, to April 24, 1979; October 22, 1980, to March 31, 1981; October 9, 1981, to May 9, 1982; September 26, 1983, to April 28, 1984; and October 17, 1985, to April 8, 1986. CBC participants missed it only twice in 25 years (1970–94) and recorded high counts of 100 or more three times: on December 27, 1988, December 27, 1989, and December 28, 1992. A higher winter count of 650 individuals was recorded in a weedy field in Cave Valley on December 20, 1963 (Wauer).

Large flocks may appear at all elevations during migration and on warm winter days. Clyde and Lois Harden and I banded a total of

238 individuals in the Watchman orchards during October 1983. And when early spring buds are available, hundreds may congregate among the cottonwoods or willows. Some of these individuals may linger until mid-May. Additionally, Jewell Gifford reported that a pair spent the entire summer of 1986 at Springdale, feeding at a chicken coop and roosting in a nearby mulberry tree.

Lesser Goldfinch. *Carduelis psaltria.*
Common summer resident and migrant; uncommon winter resident.

This little dark-backed goldfinch is present year-round, and some individuals may be permanent residents. Unlike most songbirds, this species may nest from early spring to the fall months, depending upon a reliable food supply. Jerome Gifford recorded territorial pairs on two breeding bird census plots: two pairs on a 160-acre plot in Coalpits Wash from April 15 to July 2, 1979, and two pairs on a 40-acre plot at Grafton from May 13 to July 15, 1979. In addition, John Egbert found a nest 15 feet high on a boxelder at the South Campground on June 1, 1994; Richard A. Stuart found a nest, containing two nestlings, on an oak tree in Oak Creek Canyon; and I found a very late nest in an ash tree at the ZCVC on October 29, 1963—the young left the nest on November 5.

Post-nesting birds usually congregate in large flocks and feed on weed and sunflower seeds in fields and along the roadways. These flocks usually remain in the lowlands all winter, if an adequate seed-crop is available, but numbers can be irregular. Christmas Bird Count participants recorded it on 17 of 25 years (1970–94), but totals varied from 10 or fewer on 10 years and 35 or more on eight years, including a high count of 57 on December 27, 1982.

American Goldfinch. *Carduelis tristis.*
Fairly common migrant and winter resident.

Records primarily from the lowlands extend from early September, through the winter months, to the end of May. It is most numerous from mid-October to mid-May. High fall counts include 150 at the Clear Creek Ranch on September 10, 1972 (Jerome Gifford), and 55 at Springdale on October 19, 1965 (Wauer). Christmas Bird Count participants recorded it on 19 of 25 years (1970–94), although, like the more stable Lesser Goldfinch, numbers varied from year to year:

five or fewer individuals were tallied on six years, and 35 or more were found on eight years, including a high of 87 on December 27, 1994.

Winter bird numbers remain reasonably stable until the spring migrants arrive in early April, when numbers can fluctuate from one day to the next. Although some groups linger into mid-May, the numbers are much reduced, and all depart by the end of the month. There are no June or July reports.

Evening Grosbeak. *Coccothraustes vespertinus.*
Sporadic visitor.

This colorful bird has been recorded in the Zion Park area every month but September. It is most numerous, although irregular, in the lowlands in spring from late March to mid-May, usually feeding on the abundant fresh tree buds. It is least numerous in summer, although there are a few records: I found a pair and a lone female at Lava Point on June 9, 1965, and pairs at Blue Springs Lake on June 9 and August 30, 1965; Jerome Gifford found it in Refrigerator Canyon on July 25, 1976.

Fall reports are scattered and from all elevations. It is most numerous during invasion years such as in 1963–64 when 65 were recorded on the December 1963 CBC, in contrast to none in 1962 and 1964. Also in 1963, I found flocks of 25 and 75 individuals at the East Entrance on October 24 and November 7, respectively, and 20 at Potato Hollow on October 31. And Gifford found a flock of 75 to 100 birds in a Springdale motel yard on May 15, 1964. To further illustrate its irregular occurrence, it was recorded on only nine CBCs in 25 years (1970–94), but those nine counts produced highs of 38, 72, 83, and 50 individuals in December 1973, 1987, 1989, and 1991, respectively.

FAMILY PASSERIDAE: OLD WORLD SPARROWS

House Sparrow. *Passer domesticus.*
Abundant permanent resident.

This little non-native bird is most numerous around towns and ranches, but it also occurs in the South and Watchman Campgrounds, at the NPS residential areas, and at the ZCVC. In 1981 and 1982, Jerome Gifford recorded 9 and 12 nesting pairs on a 25-acre breeding bird census plot in the Watchman Campground. Like the non-native Starling, they drive native species away by dominating nesting sites and available food supplies. And on 25 CBCs (1970–94), participants tallied an average of 110 individuals, more than 100 on 16 years, and a high count of 184 on December 28, 1992. Also of interest, these counts have significantly increased in 25 years: averages calculated in five-year categories increased from 33, 100, 142, 116, to 159, which is good evidence that this species will continue to increase and impact the park's native bird life.

Birds of Uncertain Occurrence

The following birds are not included in the regular annotated list because they need further verification; they have not been documented by either a specimen or photograph or by unquestionable reports by five or more individuals or parties.

Clark's Grebe. *Aechmophorus clarkii.*

Jerome Gifford reported that "Individuals of the *clarkii* form were at . . . Zion N.P." in spring 1985 (Kingery and Lawson 1985), and Steve Hedges reported that 10 individuals, along with 20 Western Grebes, "spent the winter" of 1988–89 at Quail Creek Reservoir (letter from Hedges).

American Bittern. *Botaurus lentiginosus.*

Angus Woodbury reported that one "spent a few days in Zion Canyon, in September, 1928" (Presnall 1935). It also was recorded at the Jesse Gifford pond in Springdale on May 18, 1975 (Jerome Gifford).

Red-shouldered Hawk. *Buteo lineatus.*

Mark Bromley and Merrill Webb reported one in Rockville during the December 27, 1982, CBC. And Bob Rhodes reported two individuals in Emerald Pools Canyon on July 15, 1995.

Broad-winged Hawk. *Buteo platypterus.*

Shane Pruett reported a "mature" bird "soaring over Oak Creek Canyon" on May 2, 1994 (NPS files).

Zone-tailed Hawk. *Buteo albonotatus.*

There are two park reports: Jan Hart found one flying over the Great West Canyon on June 26, 1993; it "soared over summit near eye level; tail banding and uplifted wings clearly visible" (NPS files). And Valeria Haan reported one with "multi-bands on tail" at Lava Point on September 1, 1994 (NPS files). There is an accepted record (by the Utah Bird Records Committee) north of Zion Park at Capitol Reef National Park for June 3, 1984, by Chris Schultz.

Sandhill Crane. *Grus canadensis.*

There are two reports: David and Margaret Mindell reported a single bird in the Watchman Campground on December 3, 1979, and Fern and J. L. Crawford and Dorothy Sousa also found one at the Watchman Area on December 27, 1994.

Black-bellied Plover. *Pluvialis squatarola.*

Jerome Gifford found a lone bird in winter plumage at the Grafton Ponds on November 27, 1981.

Long-billed Curlew. *Numenius americanus.*

Five birds were found along the Virgin River west of Grafton on March 2, 1975 (Jerome Gifford); one was seen over Interstate Highway 15 near the northwest corner of the park at Kanarraville, on September 12, 1976 (Ken Kertell and Peter Scott); and another lone bird was reported for Cave Valley in June (undated) by Janet Ellis (NPS files).

Red Phalarope. *Phalaropus fulicaria.*

Denny and Gail Davies found a dead phalarope in the Watchman Residential Area on May 22, 1994. The carcass was examined and identified by Sheri Fedorchak, who placed it in the NPS freezer; it was accidentally discarded.

Herring Gull. *Larus argentatus.*

There are four reports. The first is a lone bird seen flying over the Springdale Ponds on February 14, 1965 (Wauer). Four individuals were next reported at Springdale on March 21, 1973, by Glen Arnold and Pearl Justet. And Jerome Gifford reported it twice in the fall: one at the Kolob Reservoir on October 13, 1978, and another in the Watchman area on October 18, 1981.

Caspian Tern. *Sterna caspia.*

Seth Phalen and Peter Scott found four individuals at the Kolob Reservoir on September 11, 1974, and Jerome Gifford reported two at the Grafton Ponds on March 18, 1982.

Black Tern. *Chlidonias niger.*
There is one report: Mark Zolink and Riley Nelson observed one with a lone Forster's Tern at the Kolob Reservoir on August 13, 1981.

Inca Dove. *Columbina inca.*
Kevin Wallace reported one at Mooney's Pond in Rockville on October 12, 1986.

Short-eared Owl. *Asio flammeus.*
A specimen, without any documentation, was found in the NPS freezer; it was prepared as a study skin. And Heather Gates reported one in Kolob Canyon on July 18, 1995.

Vaux's Swift. *Chaetura vauxi.*
Lois Harden and I found one flying over the Springdale Ponds on September 11 and 13, 1965 (Wauer and Russell 1967). And Clyde Morrison reported one over the Grafton Ponds on May 13, 1985.

Blue-throated Hummingbird. *Lampornis clemenciae.*
An immature male was observed daily at hummingbird feeders in Springdale from August 3 to 8, 1972, by Jerome Gifford and Lois Harden, and a female was seen there on August 5, 1972 (Gifford).

Three-toed Woodpecker. *Picoides tridactylus.*
Jerome Gifford found a lone bird in upper Pine Canyon on January 15, 1982.

Vermilion Flycatcher. *Pyrocephalus rubinus.*
Although Vasco Tanner "noted it" within the park and there are specimens from Hurricane (Presnall 1935), and I also found it at Hurricane on four occasions (from May 11 to July 20), the only Zion Park report is one by Kris Fair, who reported one in the Watchman Campground on August 8, 1987.

Eastern Kingbird. *Tyrannus tyrannus.*

Jerome Gifford reported this eastern flycatcher on four occasions: three individuals at the East Entrance on May 13, 1964; one at Springdale on September 17 and 18, 1974; and one there on May 4, 1976. In addition, Marc Breuninger reported one near the South Campground Amphitheater on April 27, 1991.

Gray Jay. *Perisoreus canadensis.*

Christine and Jon Dick reported one in Oak Creek Canyon on December 28, 1981, during the annual CBC.

Verdin. *Auriparus flaviceps.*

The only report is a lone bird seen at a winter nest near the North Creek Pond on December 20, 1962 (Wauer).

Varied Thrush. *Ixoreus naevius.*

Bill and Sharon (last name unrecorded) found one in the Watchman Campground on April 28, 1975; it was later verified by Peter Scott.

Gray Catbird. *Dumetella carolinensis.*

Two individuals were found at the Springdale Ponds on December 16, 1975 (Jerome Gifford), and Greer Chesher reported one at the Watchman Residential Area on March 22, 1983.

Crissal Thrasher. *Toxostoma crissale.*

There are two reports: Jerome Gifford found one in Coalpits Wash on May 24, 1984, and Alan Seagert reported one at an unspecified park site on October 29, 1984.

Townsend's Warbler. *Dendroica townsendi.*

There are three reports. It was first reported above the West Rim Cabin on October 3, 1963, by Dennis Carter. Jerome Gifford observed six individuals at his Springdale feeders during a snowstorm on the upper plateau on October 18, 1971. And Nancy and Robert Dean reported a male in a mixed flock of birds (Mountain Chickadees, Red-breasted and White-breasted Nuthatches, and Brown Creepers) in Taylor Creek on October 1, 1995.

Hermit Warbler. *Dendroica occidentalis.*

V. E. Lemert reported one at "Zion on August 12, 1995" (NPS files).

Black-and-white Warbler. *Mniotilta varia.*

The first report for the Zion Park area was a female in the Watch-man Campground on August 6, 1981 (Rene Lauback). Next, a male was reported at an unspecified site on June 22, 1982 (Ray Johnson and Dan Lundeen). And Myrtle and Denver Smith reported one at the Watchman Residential Area on May 17, 1985.

Hooded Warbler. *Wilsonia citrina.*

Riley Nelson, Cathy Pasterezyk, and Mark Zolank reported a male at the Chamberlain Ranch on September 10, 1981.

Baird's Sparrow. *Amnodramus bairdii.*

Richard A. Stuart reported one in the Watchman Area on October 5, 1970. This species has never been positively documented for Utah, according to Steve Hedges.

Harris' Sparrow. *Zonotrichia querula.*

There are three reports. I found one with a large flock of White-crowned Sparrows below Rockville on December 29, 1964; Jerome Gifford reported one at the Springdale Ponds on December 29, 1973, and one at Grafton on the December 27, 1993, CBC.

Chestnut-collared Longspur. *Calcarius ornatus.*

Ken Kertell reported one in Coalpits Wash on October 10, 1974.

Snow Bunting. *Plectrophenax nivalis.*

On January 4, 1979, Glenn and Meridy Cross, Louise Excell, and Charles Torrance found a male in winter plumage on Gooseberry Mesa, south of Grafton. And Jon Dick reported one in Pine Creek in mid-January (day not recorded) 1980.

Rusty Blackbird. *Euphagus carolinus.*

A pair was seen on a willow in the open meadow below the Kolob Reservoir on June 1, 1965 (Wauer); attempts to find it the following week were unsuccessful.

Pine Grosbeak. *Pinicola enucleator.*

There are two reports: I found one at the West Rim cabin on March 31, 1965, and Jerome Gifford reported one at the East Entrance on January 29, 1977.

Purple Finch. *Carpodacus purpureus.*

Richard A. Stuart reported three individuals near the East Entrance on the December 19, 1972, CBC. The fall and winter of 1972–73 was an invasion year for the species; numerous flocks were found east of the park, including 59 tallied on the Kanab, Utah, CBC (*American Birds* 1973:479).

APPENDIX A

Bird Records Report Forms

Both Zion National Park and the Utah Bird Records Committee request your assistance in documenting all bird species that are out of their normal range.

The National Park Service is interested in all bird species recorded during visits to the Zion National Park area, especially those of "Uncertain Occurrence" or considered casual or rare. Birders are encouraged to send complete reports to the Division of Resource Management, Zion National Park, Springdale, Utah 84767-1099. Or, for individual species of importance, please submit a "Natural History Field Observation" card for each observation (sample at top of page 170). These are available at the park visitor centers on request.

In addition, the Utah Bird Records Committee also requests information on all out-of-range species found in Utah. The Utah Bird Records Committee (Utah Ornithological Society) form at the bottom of page 170 (printed with permission of the committee) is recommended.

Form 10-257
"R" 5/83

DEPARTMENT OF THE INTERIOR
NATIONAL PARK SERVICE
NATURAL HISTORY FIELD OBSERVATION

OBSERVATION:

LOCATION:

DATE *(Month, Day, Year)*	TIME *(a.m., p.m.)*	WEATHER

Description, Behavior, Number, Sketch, Map, Etc. *(use reverse if necessary)*

BE ACCURATE — DO NOT GUESS

PARK:

OBSERVER: *(include name, address, phone number)*

UTAH ORNITHOLOGICAL SOCIETY
VERIFICATION OF UNUSUAL SIGHT RECORD FOR UTAH

Common Name: _____ Scientific Name: _____

Date: _____ Time: _____ Length of time observed: _____

Number: _____ Age: _____ Sex: _____

Location: _____

Latilong: _____ Elevation (if known): _____

Distance to bird: _____ Light conditions: _____

Optical equipment: _____

Weather: _____

Description: (Write a detailed description of the bird's appearance, including size, shape, plumage pattern, color, and any unique features.)

References

American Ornithologists' Union. 1957. *Check-list of North American Birds.* Baltimore, MD: The Lord Baltimore Press, Inc.

———. 1983. *Check-List of North American Birds.* Lawrence, KS: Allen Press, Inc.

———. 1985. Thirty-fifth Supplement to the American Ornithologists' Union *Check-List of North American Birds. The Auk* 102:680–86.

———. 1989. Thirty-seventh Supplement to the American Ornithologists' Union *Check-List of North American Birds. The Auk* 106:532–38.

———. 1993. Thirty-ninth Supplement to the American Ornithologists' Union *Check-List of North American Birds. The Auk* 110:675–82.

———. 1996. Fortieth Supplement to the American Ornithologists's Union *Check-list of North American Birds. The Auk* 112:819–30.

Behle, William H. 1943. *Birds of Pine Valley Mountain Region, Southwestern Utah.* Bulletin of the University of Utah 34(2):1–85.

———. 1944. Check-list of the Birds of Utah. *The Condor* 46(2):67–87.

Behle, William H., John B. Bushman, and Clifton M. 1958. *Birds of the Kanab Area and Adjacent High Plateaus of Southern Utah.* Bulletin of the University of Utah 11(7):1–92.

Behle, William H. and Michael L. Perry. 1975. *Utah Birds: Guide, Check-list and Occurrence Charts.* Salt Lake City: Utah Museum of Natural History.

Behle, William H., E. O. Sorenson, and C. M. White. 1985. *Utah Birds: A Revised Checklist.* Salt Lake City: Utah Museum of Natural History, Occas. Publ. No. 4.

Bryant, Fred C., and Darrell Nish. 1975. Habitat Use by Merriam's Turkey in Southwestern Utah. In *Proceedings of the Third National Wild Turkey Symposium*, ed. Lowell K. Halls:6–13. Austin: Texas Parks and Wildlife Department.

Carter, Dennis L., and Roland H. Wauer. 1965. Black Hawk Nesting in Utah. *The Condor* 67(1):82–83.

Day, K. S. 1994. Observations on Mountain Plover (*Charadrius montanus*) breeding in Utah. *Southwestern Naturalist* 39:298–300.

Gifford, Jerome L. 1979a. 101. Sparse Pine-Fir Aspen Woodland. *American Birds* (January):84.

———. 1979b. 116. Farm with Ponds. *American Birds* (January):86.

———. 1979c. 131. Pygmy Forest-Chaparral. *American Birds* (January):90.

———. 1980a. 131. Ghost Town, Orchards and Pastures. *American Birds* (January):76.

———. 1980b. 138. Desert Shrub. *American Birds* (January):78.

———. 1981. 173. Slickrock Ponderosa Pine-Pygmy Forest-Chaparral. *American Birds* (January):91-92.

———. 1982a. 20. Slickrock-Ponderosa Pine-Pygmy Forest-Chaparral. *American Birds* (January):33.

———. 1982b. 35. Campground in Old Orchards. *American Birds* (January):37.

———. 1982c. 53. Farm with Ponds. *American Birds* (January):40.

———. 1983a. 28. Slickrock-Ponderosa Pine-Pygmy Forest-Chaparral. *American Birds* (January-February):36.

———. 1983b. 36. Campground in Old Orchards. *American Birds* (January-February):38.

———. 1983c. 50. Sewage Lagoons-Riparian Woodland. *American Birds* (January- February):40–41.

———. 1983d. 140. Deciduous-Coniferous North Slope. *American Birds* (January–February):90.

————. 1984a. 35. Deciduous-Coniferous North Slope. *American Birds* (January-February):44.

————. 1984b. 36. Slickrock-Ponderosa Pine-Pygmy Forest-Chaparral. *American Birds* (January-February):44.

————. 1984c. 70. Sewage Lagoons-Riparian Woodland. *American Birds* (January- February):56.

————. 1985. The Common Black-Hawk in Utah. *Utah Birds* 1(3):43–47.

————. 1986. Some Unusual Hummingbird Sightings in Utah. *Utah Birds* 2(3):65–71.

————. 1987. Birds of Zion National Park. Typed manuscript.

Grantham, H. 1936. The Brown Thrasher in Utah. *Condor* 38:85.

Grater, Russell K. 1947. *Birds of Zion, Bryce and Cedar Breaks.* Zion-Bryce Museum Bulletin. Springdale, UT: Zion-Bryce Natural History Association.

Harper, Kimball T. 1988. Quantitative Features of Zion National Park Vegetation. Draft report to National Park Service.

Hayward, C. Lynn, Clarence Cottam, Angus M. Woodbury, and Herbert H. Frost. 1976. *Birds of Utah.* Great Basin Naturalist Memoirs Number 1, Provo, UT: Brigham Young University.

Hedges, Steven P. 1985. First Documented Sighting of Acorn Woodpecker for Utah. *Utah Birds* 1(3):48–50.

Hertzler, Brent Carl. 1995. Zion Mexican Spotted Owls Observation Report Field Note Summary. Report to NPS, pp. 1–14.

Howe, Frank P. 1993. Population Monitoring of Utah Neotropical Migratory Birds in Riparian Habitats: 1992 Final Progress Report. Report to U. S. Fish and Wildlife Service, pp. 1–80.

Jehl, J. R., Jr. 1993. Observations on a fall migration of eared grebes, based on evidence from a mass downing in Utah. *Condor* 95:470–73.

Kaufman, Kenn. 1990. *Advanced Birding.* Boston: Houghton Mifflin Co.

Kingery, Hugh E. 1973a. 893. Kanab, Utah. *American Birds* 27:479.

————. 1973b. Great Basin-Central Rocky Mountain Region. *American Birds* 27(3):643–46.

————. 1974. Great Basin-Central Rocky Mountain Region. *American Birds* 27(1):91–96.

————. 1975. Mountain West. *American Birds* 29(4):885–90.

———. 1980. Mountain West. *American Birds* 34(3):293–96.

———. 1982. Mountain West. *American Birds* 36(2):201–3.

———. 1984. Mountain West. *American Birds* 38(3):339–43.

———. 1985. Mountain West. *American Birds* 39(5):942–45.

———. 1989. Mountain West Region. *American Birds* 43(2):345–47.

———. 1990. Mountain West Region. *American Birds* 44(5):1161–64.

Kingery, Hugh E., and C. S. Lawson. 1985. Mountain West Region. *American Birds* 39(3):330–33.

McDonald, Charles B., John Anderson, James C. Lewis, Robert Mesta, Allen Ratzlaff, Timothy J. Tibbitts, and Sartor O. Williams III. 1991. Mexican Spotted Owl Stria occidentalis lucida Status Review. Report to U. S. Fish and Wildlife Service, pp. 1–29.

Mindell, David P,. and Margaret H. Mindell. 1980. Wintering Raptors in the Virgin River Drainage, Southwestern Utah. Report to National Park Service, p. 1–16.

Presnall, C. C. 1935. The Birds of Zion National Park. *Proceedings of the Utah Academy of Sciences, Arts and Letters* 12:196–210.

Scott, Peter. 1975. Comment of Blue-listed Birds Occurring in Zion. Report to *NPS, pp. 1–4.*

Staats, Scott L. 1995. Monitoring Results and Survey Protocol for Ferruginous Hawks in Southwestern Utah. Utah Division of Wildlife Resources, Publ. 95-18, pp. 1–45.

Sinton, David T. 1995. Peregrine Falcon Monitoring 1995 Annual Report, Zion National Park. Report to NPS, pp. 1–14.

Tanner, Vasco M. 1927. Notes on birds collected in the Virgin River Valley of Utah. *Condor* 29:198–202.

Teresa, Shirley. 1989. Characteristics of Breeding Habitat for the Peregrine Falcon (Falco peregrinus) on the Colorado Plateau. Master's Thesis, University of California, Los Angeles.

Wauer, Roland H. 1965a. Christmas Bird Count Report. Report to NPS, pp. 1–7.

———. 1965b. Intraspecific relationship in Red-shafted Flickers. *The Wilson Bulletin* 77(4):404.

———. 1965c. Wintering Rufous-crowned Sparrows Found in Utah. *The Condor* 67(5):447.

————. 1966a. Flammulated Owl Records Following May Storms in Zion Canyon, Utah. *The Condor* 68(2):211.

————. 1966b. Eastern Phoebe in Utah. *The Condor* 68(5):519.

————. 1967. New Status for the Rufous-crowned Sparrow in Utah. *The Wilson Bulletin* 79:348–49.

————. 1968. Northern Range Extension of Wied's Crested Flycatcher. *The Condor* 70(1):88.

————. 1969. Recent Bird Records from the Virgin River Valley of Utah, Arizona, and Nevada. *The Condor* 71(3):331–35.

Wauer, Roland H., and Dennis L. Carter. 1965. *Birds of Zion National Park and Vicinity.* Zion Natural History Association.

Wauer, Roland H., and Richard C. Russell. 1967. New and Additional Records of Birds in the Virgin River Valley. *The Condor* 69(4):420–23.

Willey, David. 1995. Home-Range and Roost Habitat of Mexican Spotted Owls in Southern Utah. High Desert Research 1995, p. 1–22.

Woodbury, Angus M., Clarence Cottam, and John W. Sugden. 1949. *Annotated Check-list of the Birds of Utah.* Bulletin of the University of Utah 39(16):1–40.

Woodbury, Angus M., and Clarence Cottam. 1962. *Ecological Studies of Birds in Utah.* University of Utah Biological Series 12(7):1–33.

Zion Natural History Association. 1994. Zion National Park, Utah [map]. Utah: Zion Natural History Association.

Index